at Stanford University

50 Years of REDESIGN
(1967–2017)

Edited by
Tamara Carleton, Ph.D.

Innovation
Leadership
Publishing

Copyright © 2019
Innovation Leadership Publishing

Front cover & book theme:
Brent Campbell

Layout, graphics & back cover:
Anders Häggman

All rights reserved. No part of this publication may be reproduced, distributed, or transmitted in any form or by any means, including photocopying, recording, or other electronic or mechanical methods, without the prior written permission of the publisher, except in the case of brief quotations embodied in critical reviews and certain other noncommercial uses permitted by copyright law.

ISBN-13: 978-1-7332022-0-6

First Edition

Table of Contents

The Course		The Students		The Extras	
Learning	**3**	1960s	**89**	Course Listings	**153**
Companies	**25**	1970s	**91**	Lexicon	**163**
Teams	**37**	1980s	**99**	Publications	**167**
Loft	**53**	1990s	**109**	Network Maps	**175**
Showcase	**61**	2000s	**123**	Contributors	**191**
Global	**69**	2010s	**143**	Image Sources	**195**

Foreword
Tamara Carleton, Ph.D.

> This is a commemorative book about a year-long design course that has been taught at Stanford University since 1967. This long life speaks to the lasting impact of one course.

In 1967, Stanford Professors Jim Adams and Henry Fuchs introduced a new course as a way to provide practical experience for engineering design students, and this learning objective remains as relevant today.

The ME310 course is special in several ways. First, the course has been taught for an especially long time, as various teaching teams have led the course. How many classes can claim to be taught past 10 years, let alone 20 or even 50 years? Skimming the internet and informally surveying colleagues, I found no evidence of other such long-running classes. How has ME310 stood the test of time? And even if students may not have full awareness or academic choice, why then do companies continue participating — especially as repeat project sponsors?

A second reason that ME310 is special is that its pedagogy is designed around problem-based learning (PBL), before this area of research came into vogue. For an academic year, students work in small teams on real problems from companies, supported by faculty who serve more as coaches than as class instructors. This learning model has endured across decades and changing market demands — offering many lessons for faculty looking for an active learning approach.

Third, beyond teaching Stanford students, ME310 has built a tremendous global community that continues to grow — both within the companies and across a network of academic institutions, which have all adopted Stanford's ME310 model. ME310 has become a shared international experience, what some might even call a 'movement'. What about ME310 inspires these partners and has spawned a second wave of PBL design courses? At a fundamental level, these three reasons merit a deeper reflection.

In this book, the real reflections and stories come from the ME310 community — the instructors, students, teaching assistants, corporate sponsors, global partners, coaches, researchers, and those who have held multiple roles. Many fondly recall this class as one of the best learning experiences during their university time and in their life — and a number of alumni have found lasting friends, co-founders, and even marriage partners. Many stories are also missing from this book because these individuals have passed away, could not be reached since leaving Stanford, or just missed the window of publication.

As a note, I will refer to Stanford's academic year as 'AY', which refers to a fall start and spring end. Moreover, the course numbers have changed slightly over time: the course was launched as ME219 (AY1967 to AY1972), then listed briefly as ME201 (AY1972 to AY1975), then as ME210 (AY1975 to AY1998), and most recently as ME310 (AY1998 to now). For convenience, I will simply refer to the course as ME310 throughout the book.

Over the years, instructors have experimented with different assignments and course pacing to enhance the student learning. In 2005, Professor Larry Leifer introduced one major change, pairing Stanford student teams with international student teams, who then collaborate on a shared design problem. This practice has allowed students to also learn about the modern challenge of working as a globally distributed design team.

In terms of my experience with ME310, I did not take the course in its usual year format. Instead, I participated in one class experiment as a Stanford doctoral student — as part of a 'pop-up' student team for Panasonic. Later, I led two other class experiments, drawing from the ME310 curriculum as an instructor: co-teaching a Stanford 10-week online course for professional students and also overseeing an intensive seven-week program for Stanford summer students that mixes ME310 material with other tools. And I helped grow and structure the international network of partners around ME310 for two years, which gave me another view from the outside in.

Overall, this may be why ME310 continues to inspire others to experiment and adapt its model, year after year. But don't take my word for it — read some of the stories here from the first 50 years.

Currently CEO and Founder of Innovation Leadership Group LLC

stanford In the nine-month course ME310; Engineering Design Entrepreneurship and Innovation, student teams brainstorm, design, build, test, and create professional-quality prototype products for a sponsoring industry collaborator. This year's student projects included an eye makeup case and applicator, a grey water and black water recycling sink, a modular satellite, and a customizable dashboard for car sharing. Now in its fiftieth year, the course is a favorite among alumni, who frequently return to lend advice to students working through rigorous methods. ME310 instructor Larry Leifer, '62, MS '63, PhD '69, a professor of mechanical engineering, was among the course's first teaching assistants in the late '60s. He encourages all students to "dance with ambiguity", a trademark phrase of Leifer's that describes the class's commitment to a radically creative design process.

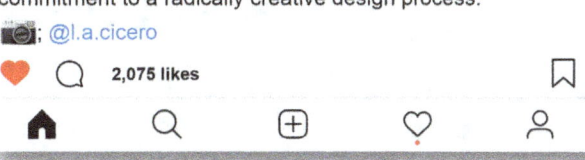; @l.a.cicero

2,075 likes

The Course

Learning

ME310 is a nine-month course, in which students work in teams to solve real problems provided by industry sponsors. Each student team addresses their problem statement (sometimes called a design brief) by designing and building a functioning prototype by June. This pedagogy is known as problem-based learning (PBL). In the safety of a class, students learn by building, by asking questions, and by embracing ambiguity. They also benefit from seeing abstract technical concepts in context. Further, ME310 helps the students to develop advanced skills in collaboration, critical thinking, and planning that later prove invaluable in their careers beyond Stanford. — *Editor*

Jim Adams, Ph.D.
ME310 faculty, AY1967–AY1970

> My reason for starting the course was based on my unhappiness with the engineering curriculum I had followed in college.

When I was in high school, I worked summers in a large machine shop, in which an uncle of mine was foreman, plus a mentor and hero. I wanted to be a tool and die maker, and the summers counted toward my apprenticeship. The shop included a dozen or so 'engineers' — all with machinist backgrounds, a few with two-year college degrees, and none with a Bachelor of Sciences degree. They were extraordinary machine designers; among other things, coming up with a series of very creative machines that made it possible to continuously cast, roll, heat treat, paint, and package Venetian blind stock.

Because of the interest of my high school counselor and good grades, I ended up as a college student at Caltech, majoring, of course, in mechanical engineering. To my disappointment, there was no hands-on material in the curriculum for us — it was all applied science and seemed to focus on solving calculus problems.

When the people in my uncle's shop (Hunter Engineering, now Hunter Douglas) found out I was now in engineering school, they made me an engineer, so now I spent my summers being paid to do what I was allegedly being trained to do. This was interesting to me, since there didn't seem to be much similarity between the two. At Caltech, we were forbidden handbooks, since things needed to be derived from 'basic' principles. Hunter Douglas engineers lived on them. Caltech loved publications. I never saw a technical paper, much less a refereed journal at Hunter Douglas. Since I had a bit of status at Caltech (e.g., highest grades in engineering in my class, student body president, etc.), I decided to fix the situation. Needless to say, I had no luck at all. Perhaps the beginning of a lifelong, low-level crusade!

When I graduated, I spent a bit of time working for Shell Oil, and then went in the U.S. Air Force (at that time the chosen alternative to carrying a rifle in Korea). I ended up in flight testing — lots of hardware; lots of things going wrong; lots of need for creativity at both Shell and the Air Force. I loved it. Then through a bunch of strange circumstances, I ended up in the art school at the University of California, Los Angeles (UCLA), as an industrial design major and loved it even more.

After running out of money at UCLA, I took a job as a designer at General Motors (also terrific), working for my favorite Caltech ex-professor (who was also a bit frustrated by their applied science leaning). He was funneling money to John Arnold, who had just come from MIT to Stanford to start a new Design Division (so named because of an instant rift between him and the then chair of Mechanical Engineering). Arnold brought three graduate students with him and was determined to build an independent program. But he was short on teachers, and I had a diploma from Caltech and experience in engineering with a year of art school as a bonus, so my GM mentor 'gave' me to Arnold.

I really liked John Arnold, Joe Pettit, the Dean then, and the younger faculty members at Stanford, but it seemed like the department was trying to copy Caltech. The 'student shops' existed, but they were staffed with elderly machinists who seemed to care more for the machines than the students, and little attention was being paid to design, development, manufacturing, and other such swell topics. Despite being a graduate student, I was immediately put to work teaching, particularly in Product Design, since Bob McKim was trying to build a program all by himself, and I had some background in the topic.

Also, by that time, I had developed an interest in trying to get engineering schools to deal with important aspects of engineering that are difficult to treat with theory – such as innovation, reliability, wear, ease of maintenance, the whole quality question — and this seemed to be a chance to try.

My first year at Stanford was fun, and during the year, I met a recruiter from NASA's Jet Propulsion Lab (JPL), who I liked a lot and helped him hire probably our most outstanding student. He then talked me into taking a summer job at JPL, which was unbelievable, because they had the job of putting together lunar spacecraft to back up U.S. President Kennedy's boast that we were going to the moon. What could be better!

I spent a couple of years traveling back and forth between JPL (making prototypes, testing, designing and building stuff that had no precedent) and Stanford (teaching and doing Ph.D. research on a project that I had begun at JPL). Stanford's Design group was getting established and hiring a few more people, but the ME curriculum did not include many important topics that I had encountered at Hunter Douglas, Shell, in the Air Force, or at General Motors.

After I got my Ph.D., I went to work full time at JPL, but stayed in touch with Stanford. In fact, one year the Design Group had a 'space year', and I fed them problems. NASA was beginning to hunt for more system engineers and engineers that were good at unprecedented hardware work (forget oiling mechanisms in space). I was put on a big NASA committee on how to fill this void, with little success, since engineering schools all seemed to have physics or math envy. However, I became friends with the professor leading the design program at Harvey Mudd College, Tom Williamson, and they did have a course in which students went through the entire process – from design through functioning hardware. In an indirect way, this may have been the predecessor of ME310.

I also met Henry Fuchs at JPL, who was then a professor at UCLA, and interested in using cases to teach engineering. I shared an office with him for a summer, and at that time John Arnold, who had become known for using fictional cases, was thinking of using real ones. I introduced them, and bingo, Henry joined the Stanford crusade. Fuchs was loads of fun (if you did not cross him) and had a good bit of industrial experience, so we plotted together through the summer.

When I joined the Stanford faculty in 1966, I decided to talk Fuchs into co-teaching a year-long course in which students in groups would design products in the autumn, worry about getting the parts made in the winter, and make the results work in the spring. It took me about two minutes to convince him of that, and we were on our way.

Currently Emeritus Professor in Mechanical Engineering at Stanford University

STANFORD BULLETIN 1972-73

Course Description

ME219A.   Advanced Engineering Design - Experience in the design of a machine. Technical requirements and interaction of various disciplines will be emphasized. The design will be carried through working drawings. Machine members will be fabricated from the drawings during Winter Quarter and the machine developed in 219C. This course and 219C constitute a series. The intent of the series is to involve the student in a major portion of the design-development process. Students should enroll for both courses. Grades will be deferred until the completion of 219C. Limited enrollment. Prerequisite: 113 or equivalent.
    3 units, Autumn

ME219B.   Design Operations - Synopsis of operations common to many design projects followed by more detailed study of case histories of design projects from various environments. Planning the experimental development of a design produced in 219A or of an approved alternate. Prerequisite: consent of instructor.
    3 units, Winter

ME219C.   Experimental Development Engineering - Testing and improvement of the design produced in 219A or approved alternate. Limited enrollment. Prerequisite: 219A or B, or consent of instructor.
    3 units, Spring

Design Division Faculty, circa mid-1970s

Henry Fuchs, Ph.D.
ME310 faculty, AY1967–AY1971

> The MechE sequence 219 A-B-C was started in 1967 by Professor Jim Adams and the author to provide graduate students with an opportunity to learn more about design.

[*Henry Fuchs gave these remarks at the American Society for Engineering Education annual meeting in June 1970 — Editor*]

As everybody has his own definition of design, it should be stated that when the author says 'engineering design', he usually means the conception and production of plans which can be executed by others to produce engineering systems or devices. This course attracts about 20 graduate students each year. Many of them are at Stanford only one year. Their backgrounds vary from recent graduates with no previous exposure to design to men with several years of diversified design experience in small companies. In such an environment, the teacher does not transmit knowledge but helps the students to learn from each other, from their work, from customers and suppliers, from catalogs, and from books. To ease the shock of transition to this mode of school work, the author started this year by the very abbreviated introduction to the theory of design shown in 'Questions for Designers' and 'Thoughts for Designers'.

We assume that our students have been exposed to plenty of analysis and that they have received the message about creativity. We know that usually they do not appreciate that most mistakes are made in defining problems, not in solving them, and that most product engineering effort must be spent in developing the prototype, not in conceiving it. We want to remedy this by or attempt at realism. We understand that the university environment is, and probably must be, unfavorable to the attempt. But we try anyhow because we want our students to get a fair idea of design before they look for a job in design or for a job in which they will work with design engineers. We also want to give them a chance to make their early mistakes in school rather than on the job. Perhaps most of all, we want to give our students a chance to taste the thrill of developing a real working device from their ideas.

The general plan of the course is this:

In Autumn, the students choose from a selection of design tasks for which we have lined up customers. Each group defines its task with the customer, produces ideas for solutions, and works out one idea to the point where it can be produced from their plans.

In Winter, the plans are executed: components procured and parts are made according to the specification and drawing. The students may meanwhile study design and development in ME219B by discussing engineering cases.

However, 219B has not been a mandatory part of the sequence. Many students have elected to take another course while the parts for their design were being made or procured.

At the beginning of Spring, the parts and components are supposed to be ready. The groups of students then assemble their designs, test them, and improve or develop them for more perfect performance or easier manufacture.

It has not worked the way we planned it. The best we have been able to do was to get the first working models ready by the end of the school year. Actually, only two of the four devices from 1968–69 really worked. The other two had to be revised and improved by other students in the following school year.

This year's projects (in 1969–70) were:
- An instrumented trailer for testing the road holding behavior of racing tires ($400 without instruments)
- An indexing table providing constant short indexing time and adjustable dwell time ($350)
- A carrier and latch mechanism to be used with timing devices for oceanographic trawling ($150)
- Redesign of the housing for an electronic sensor which permits blind people to feel the shape of printed letters (customer funded without cost limit).

The last of these could be iterated as planned because it was a more modest project starting from a working device and because the customer took care of prototype procurement. The first one just barely was finished, without checkout of the instrumentation. The other two produced working prototypes but not devices developed by iteration and re-iteration.

We are now encouraging the students to take the entire sequence of three courses. The middle quarter can then be used partly for more rigorous follow-up on the procurement of parts and partly for case discussions. The experience of a single project may be exaggerated out of proportion or rejected as exceptional. This is the reason for supplementing the direct experience of one project by vicarious experience with about ten engineering case histories. The story of the Mariner solar panel deployment shows, for instance, that even highly sophisticated spacecraft designers start out with more complex designs than they need, and that they must build hardware to evaluate designs.

We are giving up hope for completion of the hardware before the end of the school year. We may give our students appreciation for the necessity of development by letting them see the previous year's hardware in the hands of our customers and letting them hear what the customers say about it.

That we have customers for our devices turns out to be an advantage. Our students obtain feedback on the performance of the devices and learn the difficulty of obtaining reasonably clear and feasible specifications. This is one of the blessings of poverty. We would not seek customers if our school had money for building hardware. This has been our experience to date with a graduate design course. It has had many troubles but we feel it was worthwhile.

Fuchs passed away in 1989

Robert Piziali, Ph.D.
ME310 faculty, AY1975

It was a great way to provide a valuable overview of the design process combining classroom teaching with hands-on experience. I am slightly amazed that it has lasted 50 years.

Currently Principal Engineer of Biomechanics at Exponent Inc.

Questions for Designers

What is the problem?

Have I absorbed enough information?
Is it reliable?
Is it first-hand?

Have I found the most important criteria?
Are they expressed in terms which can be used? (operational)
Will they serve to examine and improve my designs?

Do I have enough different solutions to choose from?
Are they different enough?
Have I given my preconscious enough chances to suggest solutions?
Have I iterated often enough?

Can I explain my solution without handwaving?
Are my reasons documented?

How do I get the parts and components?
Are they specified clearly enough?
Any alternatives?
How much effort will it take to specify sufficiently?
How much time to procure?
How much money?

Have I tried to foresee all obstacles?
Do I have margins for the unforeseen?
Can I test before completion?
Will it be difficult to make corrections?

APPENDIX 3

Bernie Roth, Ph.D.
ME310 faculty, fall 1972, AY1991

> One of the largest motivations for me, when the Design faculty started talking about creating a three-quarter design course, was the fact that we were going to team-teach the class, and I would get to see more about what my colleagues did.

Each member of the Design Division faculty would take charge of a few lectures and use those to bring his specialty to the students. In those days my specialty was kinematics of machines and mechanisms. We were going to launch the class in the Autumn of the 1972–73 academic year, and I was going to be on leave for the Winter and Spring quarters.

I thought the Autumn quarter went well, and I remember coaching a project that Paul Hait, the founder of Pemmican Brand Beef Jerky, had sponsored for designing a new type of flexible notebook binding system. By the time I returned the following September, the structure had basically changed, and the course had become primarily run by Jim Adams.

The idea to charge corporate sponsors for projects came in an informal Design Division faculty meeting with Tom Woodson. Tom was a design professor at Harvey Mudd, who had written an introductory textbook about engineering design (T. T. Woodson, *Introduction to Engineering Design*, McGraw Hill, 1966). Tom told us that Harvey Mudd charged sponsors $1,000 for each undergraduate project. So, we thought we'll charge sponsors $2,000 for our graduate student projects.

Some years later Jim moved on to other things, and Phil Barkan took over the course. Under Phil, the course became the heart of the Design Division's Industrial Affiliates program. Companies paid to be affiliates, and their primary benefit in return was to become a sponsor of one of the course projects. A portion of this affiliate income was used to supplement the Design Division's operating budget. In return, most Division faculty coached one or more projects. I enjoyed this and looked forward to coaching one or two projects each year. This worked unevenly, and Phil was not thrilled with the system. The faculty coaching kept getting less and less, and by the time Larry Leifer took over from Phil, both the Affiliates program and the faculty coaching were on their last legs, and essentially over.

With Larry in charge of the course — and later Larry and Mark Cutkosky — my participation became giving one hybrid kinematics-and-creativity lecture each year, plus occasional coaching to work with teams having interpersonal difficulties. One year, Larry went on sabbatical, and I taught the course with of David Radcliffe, a visiting professor from Australia. It was a great experience.

Currently Professor of Mechanical Engineering at Stanford University

David Radcliffe, Ph.D.
ME310 faculty, AY1991

> The major emphasis was on the early and rapid prototyping of design ideas into hardware, culminating in a working prototype demonstrated to the project sponsors on Affiliates Day.

In 1991–92, while Larry Leifer was on sabbatical leave, ME210 was co-taught by Bernie Roth and myself, when I was a visiting scholar from the University of Queensland, Australia. We shared the responsibility for the first two quarters, and then I taught the final quarter while Prof. Roth was in France. Our students performed well in the national Lincoln Foundations Students' Engineering Design Competition winning Best of Program, one of two Silver Awards, one of the three Bronze awards and two of the four Merit Awards.

To set the tone, each quarter commenced with a one-day design exercise created to provide an experience of issues that were likely to arise in the industry project during that quarter. The most memorable of these was the Bodiometer exercise. Under severe time pressure, using Lego, cardboard, string and tape and such like, the student teams designed, prototyped and tested a hand-held device that had to accurately measure a wide range of bodily dimensions. Each team then disassembled their device and prepared a set of manufacturing instructions for its production, plus a user's manual. The competition culminated in the teams building and operating a Bodiometer designed by another group and points were awarded for the build time and measurement accuracy.

In 1991–92, there were 13 projects, and the Affiliates included Boeing, Ford, GM, FMC, Peterbilt, NASA, Hughes and Varian. The Affiliates fee was $15,000. The Peterbilt projects involved having the full-sized cabin of one of their prime movers in the ME210 room (then on the top floor of the Terman building). Bernie Roth added several degrees of difficulty to the traditional 'paper bike' project by including a circumnavigation of the pond next to the former Terman building as part of the race circuit. Many soggy bikes did not survive this most severe of tests!

I created some new classroom exercises around decision making, refined the format of student presentations, and introduced a framework for student reflection on the design process. The reflection piece was trying to counter the pervasive tendency of engineers to be action-oriented, always driving forward to the solution, and correspondingly not taking the time to stop, to review, to reflect and thus to learn from the experience of design; to be aware of, to capture and to analyze the many 'critical incidents' that occur during the course of a project — those 'ah-ha' moments. Basically we built in some structured approaches in the rhythm of the course to cause the students to capture these critical learning episodes and to take the time to extract lessons about design and about themselves from these.

One fun innovation was the introduction to the very British tradition of having 'afternoon tea' in the class sessions. This stemmed from me being Australian, and one of the TAs [*Teaching Assistants — editor*] that year being Margo Brereton, originally from the U.K. Each team was responsible for organizing light refreshments on a given afternoon. Trouble was the whole thing became VERY competitive with teams striving to outdo each other — from six-foot sandwiches to margaritas.

Currently Epistemology Professor Emeritus of Engineering Education at Purdue University

Larry

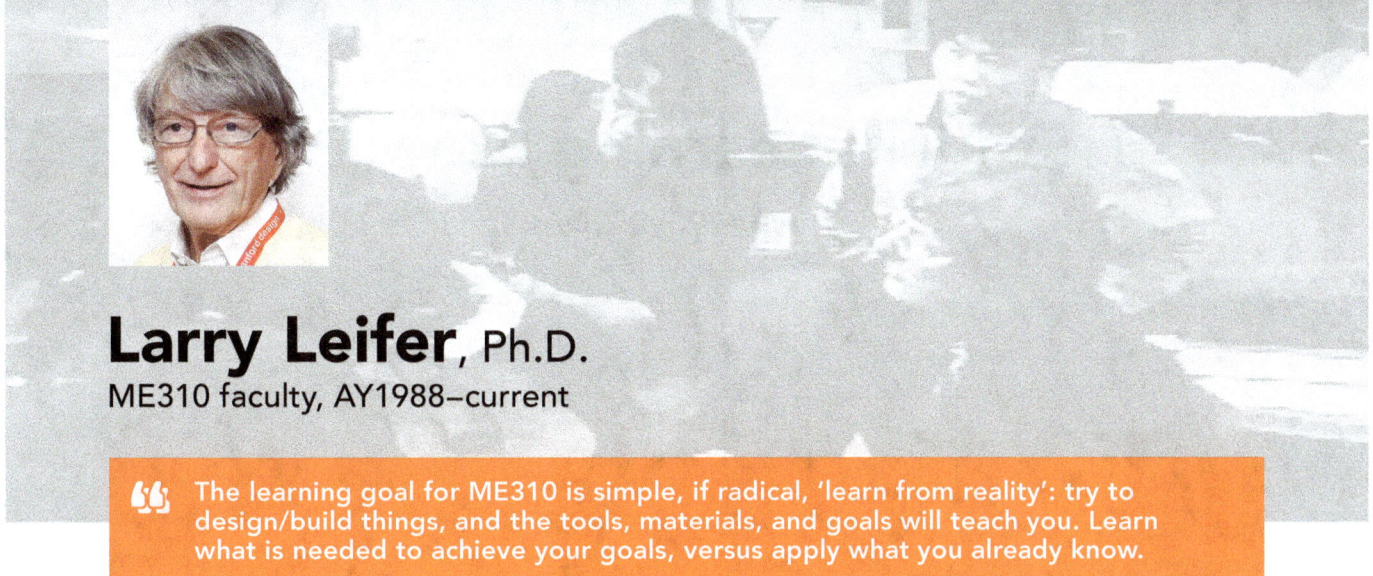

Larry Leifer, Ph.D.
ME310 faculty, AY1988–current

> The learning goal for ME310 is simple, if radical, 'learn from reality': try to design/build things, and the tools, materials, and goals will teach you. Learn what is needed to achieve your goals, versus apply what you already know.

I had been one of the first teaching assistants in the course that preceded ME210, which was taught by Earnest (Ernie) Chilton and Jim Adams. An early sponsor was SRI, an industry consulting think tank, which brought industry projects to the class. For me, Ernie was the curriculum driver and Adams the facilitator.

In the early years, we were effectively doing Project Based Learning (PBL) catch-up to entire universities that went down the PBL path (such as Aalborg, a split off from the University of Copenhagen as I recall; I visited Aalborg and was disappointed that professors were making up the problems/projects — and not drawing them from the real world of industry).

In my early academic decades, I learned that I am inclined to hunt, which is an apt metaphor for learning. Today this translates to learning from reality, what I could really imagine and build with available tools and materials. A decade of working in the field of 'rehabilitation engineering' taught me that the technology was the easy part and that the teams of engineers, clinicians, and patients were the hard part. My concurrent research in the School of Medicine's Neurology department taught me that those hot little lab computers helped us do research that was not previously possible. In my case, count muscle action potentials by computer rather than by eyeball (not feasible and no one had even tried). I took the minicomputer opportunity to our Design Group (formerly called the Design Division) to launch what is now called ME218, 'Smart Product Design'. The course is an interesting example of research technology invading the curriculum. Forty-plus years of design thinking research was born with the guiding question: 'What are engineering designers doing when they do design?' and 'Can we help them?' It was already clear from the rehab engineering days that they need help, especially when even seeking to know what the patient/user needed.

There are many more reflections. One of the most notable from last year's experience is to realize how radical ME310 is in emphasizing and demanding that students learn to 'COLLABORATE' in the wild, versus what most formal education is doing to promote and judge as 'COOPERATION'.

Currently Professor of Mechanical Engineering at Stanford University

Student Learning Process
(circa 1990–2010s)

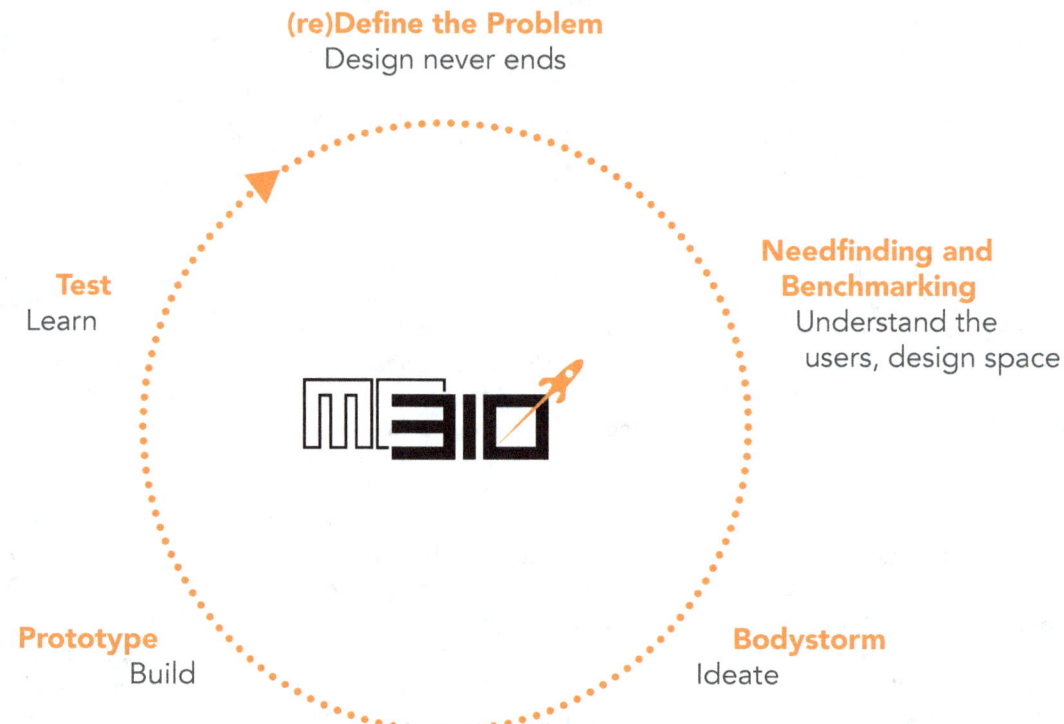

(re)Define the Problem
Design never ends

Needfinding and Benchmarking
Understand the users, design space

Bodystorm
Ideate

Prototype
Build

Test
Learn

What Teams Actually Experience

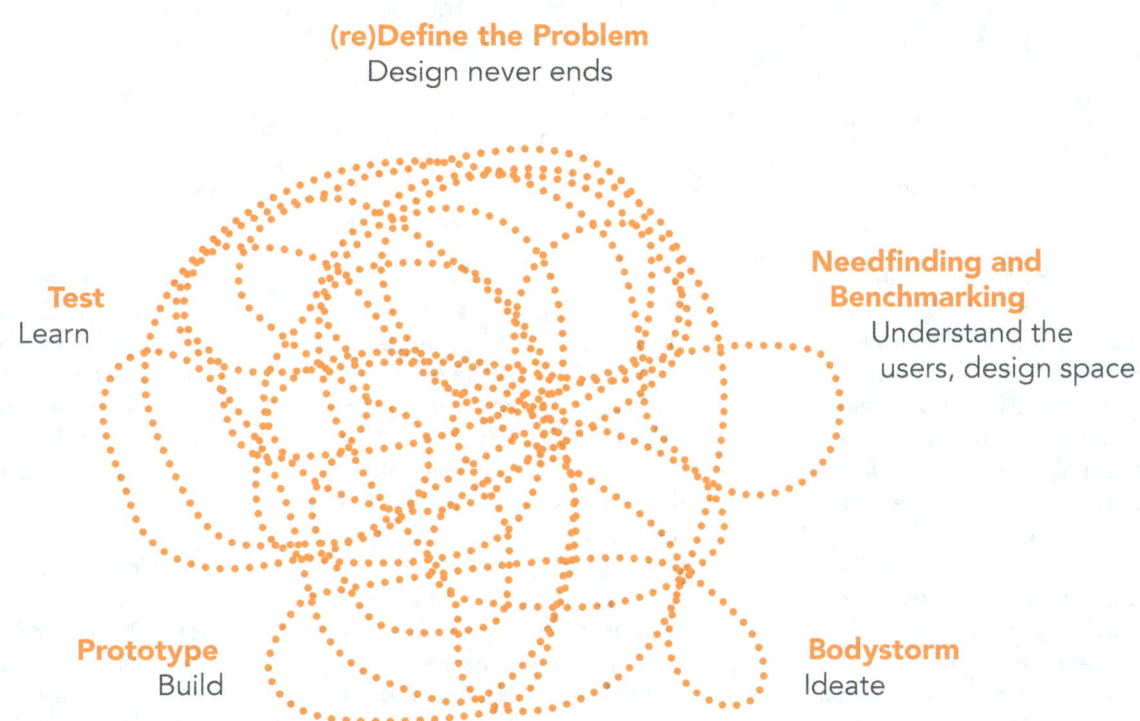

(re)Define the Problem
Design never ends

Needfinding and Benchmarking
Understand the users, design space

Bodystorm
Ideate

Prototype
Build

Test
Learn

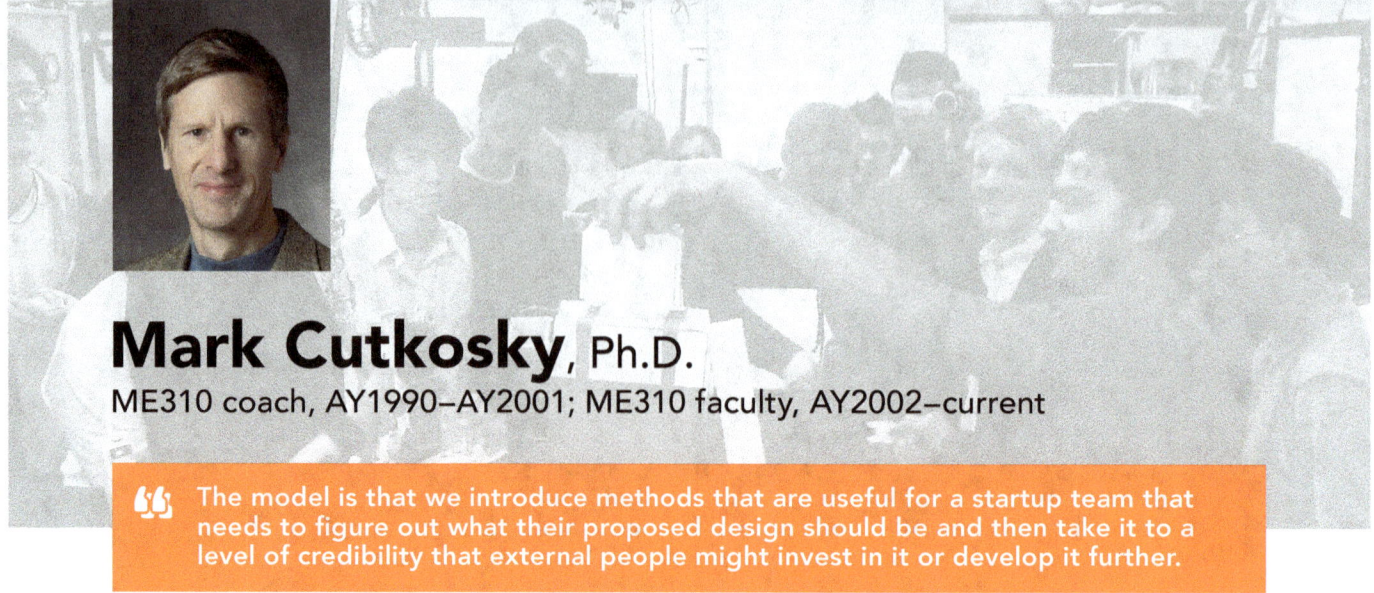

Mark Cutkosky, Ph.D.
ME310 coach, AY1990–AY2001; ME310 faculty, AY2002–current

> The model is that we introduce methods that are useful for a startup team that needs to figure out what their proposed design should be and then take it to a level of credibility that external people might invest in it or develop it further.

I first became involved when ME310 was still ME210. When I first interviewed at Stanford in 1985, the Mechanical Engineering Department did a clever thing: they invited me to attend the final spring presentations from ME210. I was very impressed, as I had never seen a class with such high-quality projects. It was one of the deciding factors that brought me to Stanford.

There are several unique elements, some that apply both to the older ME210 and some particular to the newer ME310:

- ME310 starts with very open problem statements. There is no expectation of what the design should be — it is for the teams to determine and propose what they should design, and then build it and test it.
- ME310 helps teams to understand that they can learn anything they need to bring their designs to fruition. Teams initially have a tendency to avoid designs that require expertise they lack. However, a wonderful aspect of being in Silicon Valley, with a rich network of alumni, is that we can help them find experts in almost any topic. They can talk with those people and learn what they need to know. The way I explain this to teams is: 'Take the design in whatever direction it wants to go, not the directions you are comfortable with at present.'
- ME310 is ultimately about producing a believable prototype. We expect a level of fit and finish and material construction that it doesn't take much imagination to understand what a product will look like. There is enough time and budget in the ME310 process that final manufacturing can be completed.

The content elements include corporate benchmarking and context, identifying users and other stakeholders and their needs, and lots of prototyping of ideas, pieces of solutions and eventually systems that could address the identified needs. We have some lectures to introduce topics, but the material doesn't sink in until students try it on their own. A lot of the teaching is really coaching. For me, working with ME310 teams is sometimes like mentoring my own Ph.D. students in my lab and sometimes like serving on the technical advisory board of a small company. Using my experience, I can suggest ideas, approaches, etc., that may prove useful.

Ultimately, teams are free to ignore the advice they get (and sometimes they have good reasons for doing so). But I do tell them that if multiple members of the teaching team are suggesting something, they should be pretty sure they know what they are doing before ignoring that advice.

As the projects themselves

have become more open ended, the teaching has changed. We spend more time understanding the corporate context, trends, and user needs than we did in the past. We necessarily have a bit less time to focus on technical details. We also find that lectures are less effective than in the past. Now they are mainly just to introduce a topic. The teaching is about in-class and out-of-class exercises.

For me, the most magical moment is always when a team realizes what the real contribution of their project is. They discover how to tell the story about what the design is, how it works, and why it is useful as a valid solution to a problem. This often doesn't happen until spring quarter, although we get glimpses of it along the way.

Currently Professor of Mechanical Engineering at Stanford University

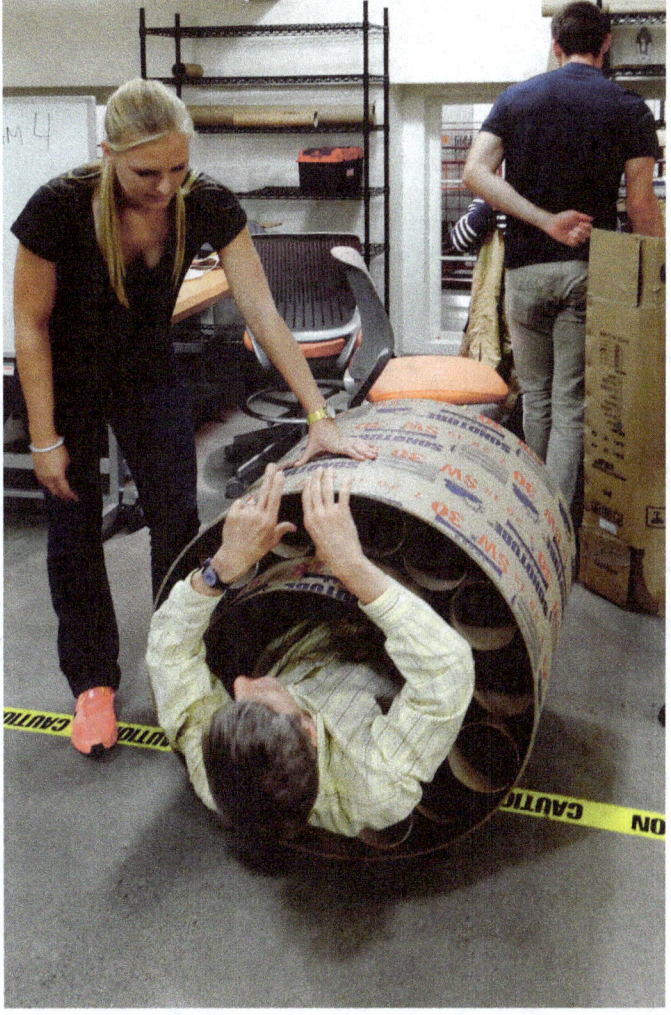

Reinhold Steinbeck
ME310 liaison for Latin America, AY2007–current

> Project-Based Learning (PBL) is well known as a methodology to promote more active learning among students. What makes ME310 unique among PBL programs is its strong focus on coaching and global teamwork.

I started getting involved with ME310 as part of the first team of the Stanford Learning Lab, working with Larry Leifer and George Toye. I believe it was 1998. I am also the founder and board member of the International Association of Problem-Based Learning and Active Learning Methodologies (PAN-PBL), so I believe in the benefits of the PBL learning model.

As the Buck Institute of Education (BIE), one of the leading organizations promoting PBL, puts it: 'Project Based Learning can be transformative for students. By presenting students with a mix of choice and responsibility, cognitive concepts and practical activities, within an environment of real-world authenticity, projects engage students in learning that is deep and long-lasting.'

The ME310 course certainly fits that definition of PBL very nicely. The very first phrase of the course description reads: 'Reality is the best teacher' — emphasizing the fact that students in ME310 take on real-world design challenges brought forth by global corporate partners. Other program elements are also reflected in a recent course description: 'The best teachers are coaches' and 'The best crucial learners are in teams of 3–4 persons'.

At the PBL2018 International Conference, two items stood out for me. The first paper was by Benjamin Bloom, one of America's leading education psychologists and most famous for 'Bloom's Taxonomy', a framework to promote higher forms of thinking. In 1984, Bloom published a paper in learning science called 'The 2 Sigma Problem: The Search for Methods of Group Instruction as Effective as One-to-One Tutoring'.

In a nutshell, Bloom's 2 Sigma work showed that students who are tutored or coached one-to-one or in small groups perform two standard deviations ('2 sigma') better than students in conventional classrooms.

People and interactions are decisive elements of the ME310 program, and the value of guidance and formative feedback provided by the coaches and industry liaisons is illustrated creatively by a student quote from Pontificia Universidad Javeriana. The student said that, in ME310, 'you start with closed eyes and then you go out and you can see the sunshine. But sometimes that sunshine blinds you, because it's so strong, and you go ahead, but you can't see everything you have to see. So in that moment, those people appear and give you sunglasses. And then you can observe everything better'.

The second paper is by

Harvard economics professor Richard Freeman. Freeman has an interesting study on diversity in science. He found that published scientific research receives greater attention if the authors are ethnically diverse. Papers that received the most citations and the most prestige — and hence were considered more innovative and relevant — were often written by a mix of people with different backgrounds. It is much better to have people collaborating when they are across different laboratories, across different parts of the U.S., between countries, rather than people only working in the same group.

With ME310's extraordinary coaching support, as well as its emphasis on diverse global teamwork, the program offers a PBL experience that encourages deeper learning and cultivates group creativity.

Currently Managing Director of IntoActions LLC

George Toye, Ph.D.
ME310 faculty, AY2007–current

> It made sense to become the testbed for this digital exploration: how to capture and reuse design knowledge in real-time, enable impromptu personal video conferencing, and facilitate document sharing and joint authoring.

The foundation of ME310's global team collaboration curriculum is rooted in its role in a DARPA research project at Stanford's Center for Design Research in the early 1990s, with Mark Cutkosky and Larry Leifer as the project's co-PIs. Back then, the internet (i.e., information super-highway) and, in particular, the world wide web (WWW) were primarily available to the research community, and DARPA had interest in exploring how these facilities could foster advances in integrated design and manufacturing processes upon public availability of the internet. For ME210/310, such entry opportunity to an internet-based infrastructure prompted a course redesign.

Going fully digital with documentation brought about the design of documentation templates that promoted valuable, pedagogically-motivated organization and structure. And thus begat ME310's end-of-quarter document template and the strategy of how each would be iteratively updated every quarter. These have been refined but remained fundamentally similar through 25 years.

In those early days, Stanford's video group recorded popular graduate engineering (lecture-based) courses and offered these recordings to staff at Silicon Valley companies via live remote satellite TV broadcasts (via SITN — Stanford Instructional Television Network). Though ME310 is not a lecture-based course, but as means to begin exploring remote collaborations, we decided to offer the course to SITN subscribers. Along with some Bay Area takers who could come to campus, we had one HP student located in Massachusetts who signed up. That student team would video conference cross-country using Cornell University's CUseeMe — the first such experimental tool available for personal computers. Unlike the relatively simple-to-use video conference tools we can use today, tools in those days (like CUseeMe) were more complex and definitely quirky; they barely worked — requiring typically a half hour or more of tweaking just to hear/see the other side with stability of a few minutes.

One early observation was that the remote students were not regularly using these tools and facilities due to limited computer and network access. While there were computer labs on campus and clusters in the ME310 loft, few students had personal computers. For those who did, internet access was through 1200 bps dial-up modem. 'Portable' computing was very much in its infancy.

Understanding that students

liked mobility and often desired to do work outside the ME310 loft, ME310 invested in purchasing early-generation Apple Macintosh Powerbooks, one for each team. We wired up the loft with ample convenient plug-in AppleTalk/PhoneNet outlets for faster networking. While students' computer tools use increased, adoption remained lighter than desired. The Powerbooks were a team-shared resource, mostly locked in the cabinet under each team's table; no team member could count on having possession or using their Powerbook at non-pre-scheduled times. The cost of providing every student with computers was prohibitive. Thankfully over time, cost and performance considerations for personal wireless mobile computing have improved and such technologies are now ubiquitous. Notable for me: ME310 was there at the leading (bleeding) edge — a quarter century ago.

My deep involvement in ME310 came about through this DARPA project for which I had the role of being the local ME310 tech lead. ME310 was the first course at Stanford to have its own website on the internet — running on our own dedicated Linux server with a 'fast' 25Mhz Intel 486 processor. We created our own web-based file repository software for collecting and archiving student documents.

ME310 teaching assistant Jack Hong was instrumental in creating the 'Personal Electronic Notebook w/Sharing' (PENS) software to allow group-based publication of integrated text/graphics (for creating notes, screenshots, sketches and organizing ideas) onto the internet to be shared informally among team members. This work resulted in a U.S. patent: 'Hyper-text document transport mechanism for firewall-compatible distributed world-wide web publishing' (#US5710883A). With PENS (functionally similar and a predecessor to blogs), we were already addressing issues/policies regarding privacy of internet published content — privacy remains to be a haunting concern in today's internet use. Later, Tao Liang, ME310 alumnus and Ph.D. student, developed the first version of the Web Shop software enabling Stanford students to check the availability and reserve machine use times at another Stanford lab (PRL) online.

One off-books [stealth] story that few are aware of: in 1994 our ME310 Linux server was also home for about 6 months to an experimental Chinese dinner menu ordering with on-campus delivery service for graduate students. Today, online food ordering and delivery is commonplace via waiter-on-wheels, etc.

Another year, the shared network drive of the entire class was found completely wiped clean. No one involved in the class could account for the drive's content loss. A thorough investigation over several days failed to find evidence of any external hacker intrusion. Ultimately, we discovered that the respective user's computer had been hacked based on a trivial password.

My takeaway: we learn, and we evolve. Sometimes the journey that helps us learn is more bumpy, less predictable than enjoyable; the more painful the journey, the more memorable the lesson. ;-) This is all part of the ME310 pedagogy of learning from live experience. The world is constantly changing. Hence we must continue to adapt, be open to learn — not only more but anew.

Currently Adjunct Professor in Mechanical Engineering at Stanford University

Companies

Much of ME310's format and unique appeal relies on the corporate partners each year. They sponsor projects for various reasons, often seeing the students as an external R&D unit or as a special incubator team. In the early years of ME310, companies proposed more technically-driven problems, such as devising a new type of flow measuring mechanism. In recent years, companies have broadened their challenges to encompass topics of service, innovation, and emerging technologies. Corporate liaisons support the students' learning journey throughout the academic year and see the final result at a year-end "demo day" — called Design EXPErience (EXPE for short) in recent years. — *Editor*

Jim Adams, Ph.D.
ME310 faculty, AY1967–AY1970

> **"** There were initial difficulties launching the course. The then department chair of Mechanical Engineering and many of the faculty members were not excited (to say the least) about the idea.

The people in charge of the shops were used to having students build simple things from a drawing they would furnish, and we had to find customers who would support the costs involved. So we began with people we knew. I only remember some of the specific details. One of our first customers was Bob Moffatt, who had spent a lot of time at General Motors before earning his Ph.D. at Stanford and joining the faculty. He was very supportive of our attempt and furnished some research money to build him an apparatus that would circulate fluids in various modes. The U.S. Veteran's Administration took us on to design and build a Braille trainer, which passed Braille printed on a tape under the users' fingers at various speeds. I remember pursuing work from JPL, GM, and NASA Ames, and we got the shops turned around, a problem finally solved by hiring the incomparable David Beach. Henry Fuchs and I were both delighted with the student output.

Henry and I loved teaching the course, because we both had a lot of experience in areas in which design was merely the tip of the problem and had experience with designs that didn't work very well (if at all) when first assembled. We also both loved machines and were fascinated with common problems that seem to be beyond logic. I still get great pleasure coming across seemingly sophisticated and complex mechanisms, that when first assembled, 'bind'. Such things reminded me of times in my past, such as when the prototype of a particular advanced fighter that was built to feature the then-new 'Gatling gun', which delivered a very high rate of fire, was brought to Edwards Air Force Base to be tested, only to demonstrate that when fired, the vibration would cause the engine to flame out.

I also remember Henry spellbinding JPL during his summer by building a dyna-focal mount to separate spacecraft, which are relatively delicate, from the horrendous vibration associated with a launch. Such suspension systems work by conventional damping through most frequencies, and picking up additional friction during large excursions, this one by picking up dampers that were engaged through pins in slots. On the big day, his prototype mount, with attached instrumented test spacecraft, was bolted to the shake table, and the simulated launch vibration turned on. Everyone agreed that his mount made the most noise of anything ever tested at the lab. It worked, but I learned something again. Brilliance must be compatible with the company culture. Spacecraft are supposed to be extremely sophisticated, and not make extremely loud clattering noises.

As a good ending to the story, on the wall of my office hangs a beautifully made and extremely lightweight damper that another friend of mine and I caused to be added late in the development cycle to the first Venus spacecraft in order to decrease launch vibration on a critical instrument. Heroic, we thought, except we had to hide from the structural designers for a while because we had put point damping into a structure they loved because it depended entirely on distributed damping. Needless to say, our 'fix' flew and operated beautifully. It would have been a great problem for ME310.

Currently Emeritus Professor of Mechanical Engineering at Stanford University

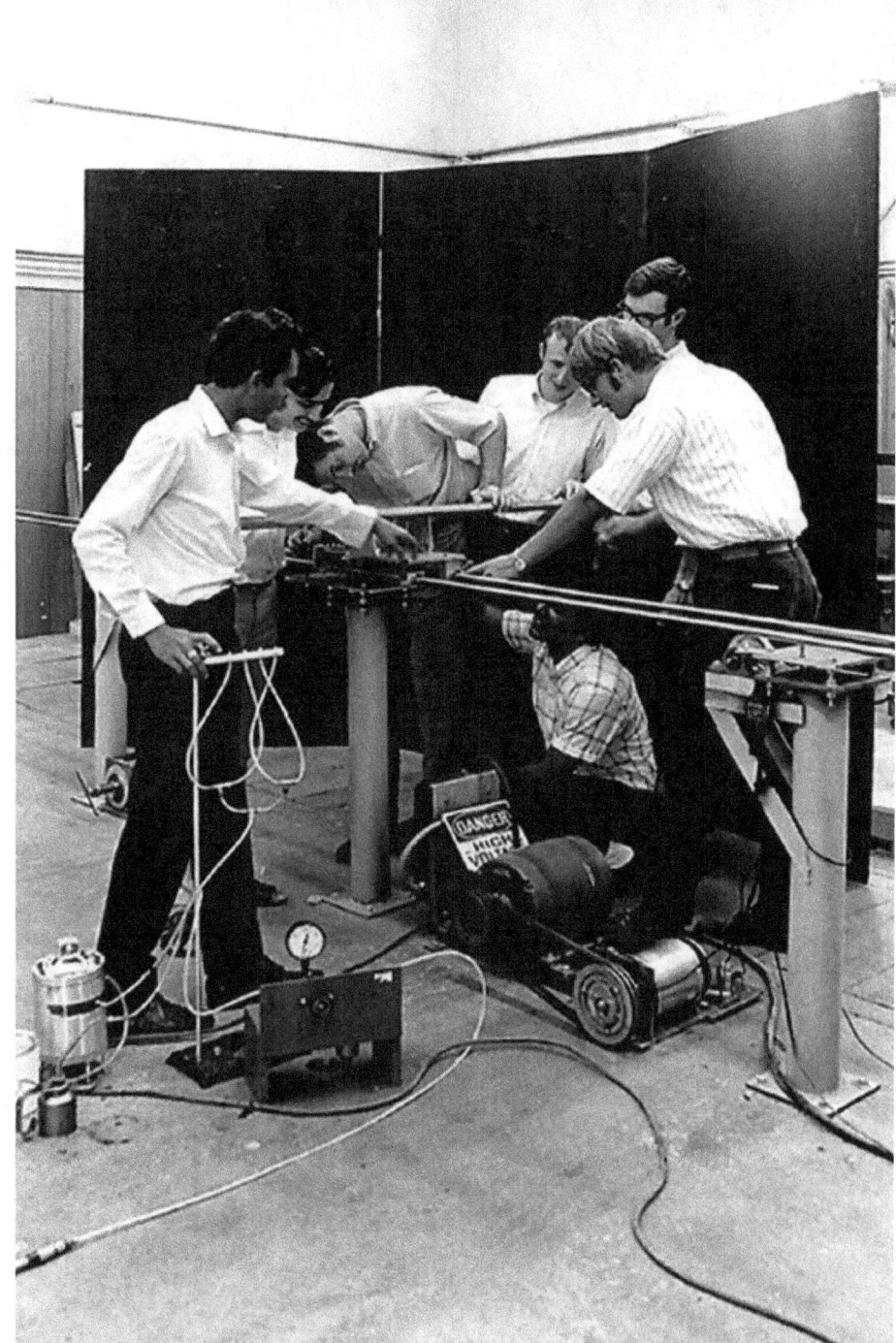

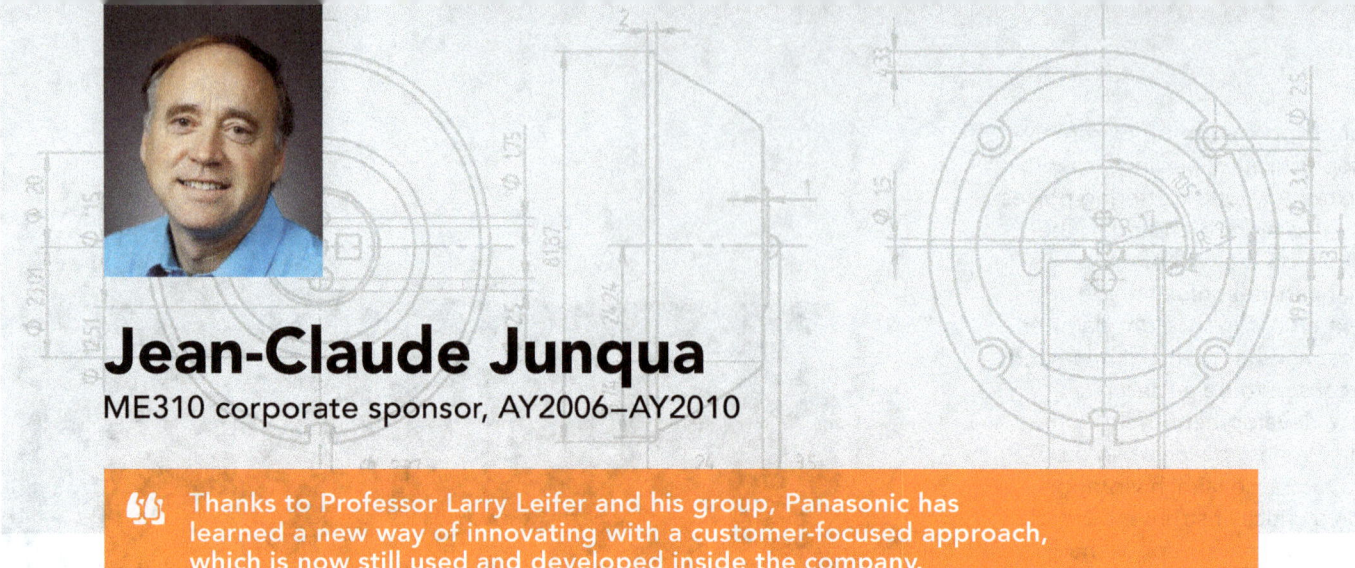

Jean-Claude Junqua
ME310 corporate sponsor, AY2006–AY2010

> Thanks to Professor Larry Leifer and his group, Panasonic has learned a new way of innovating with a customer-focused approach, which is now still used and developed inside the company.

Panasonic became involved in ME310 after its research lab (Panasonic San Jose Laboratory) was established in 2006. This involvement came from the recognition that while technology was an essential piece towards the success of the company, innovation was moving towards a customer-focused process illustrated by the design approach that was pioneered by Professor Larry Leifer and his group with the ME310 program.

After being involved in this program, which at the beginning appeared messy and difficult to duplicate, it became clear that the ideas and concepts that were generated were quite different from the technology focused approach that was often pursued in the company. Working together with multi-disciplinary teams, rapid prototyping and working on prototypes to obtain user feedback to guide the next steps of the journey were quite new for many of the engineers. At first, though there was some level of resistance from some groups in the company, the speed at which new ideas were created and visualized in a tangible form attracted a strong level of interest in the company.

We really started to make good progress in introducing innovation based on design principles when we were awarded the best of show at CEATEC in Japan in 2008 for a remote control called EzTouch that started from hints obtained from a remote control project done in collaboration with the ME310 program. At this time some of the press mentioned that it was the first time that they saw a Japanese company innovating the Apple way. From there on design thinking was taken seriously in the company, propagated in Japan and Europe, and adopted as a way to create speed and innovative concepts in the company.

Currently CEO & founder of CE2Innovate

Deanna Wilkes-Gibbs
ME310 corporate sponsor, AY2006–AY2010

ME310 was an early part of our Panasonic Silicon Valley lab's transition from being focused on more traditional R&D to its emergence as a center for innovation at Panasonic. It was also important in my personal journey to a place where I am able to 'dance with ambiguity' so much more comfortably than before. These days, design thinking principles still inform much of what I do. It all began in the early 2000s with Larry Leifer, Mark Cutkosky, and our FutureFlat project — the first of many ME310 projects with which I was closely involved, often meeting weekly with the teams. I have many fond memories — such as the EXPE conversation in which several of us gleefully brainstormed a name for the global component: SUGAR!

Currently consulting

Guidelines for a Student Challenge
(circa 1990–2010s)

ME310 Partner Project Prompt

What is a Partner Project Prompt?

This is the problem/opportunity statement that is developed by a partner company and given to ME310 Students at the beginning of the academic year. This is the starting point (not the ending point) of the design exploration process.

What is an example of a Partner Project Prompt?

Consumer electronic products waste is a significant and growing problem leading to increasing government regulation of "end of life" disposal regulations. The design challenge is to develop a modular, fully recyclable consumer electronic product that can be easily and safely disassembled by the consumer at the product end-of-life while leveraging as much as possible the primary recycling methods available to consumers today.

What are the characteristics of a good Partner Project Prompt?

Partner Project Prompts are usually two sentences:

- **Sentence #1:** concisely describes the problem and/or market opportunity
- **Sentence #2:** states the design challenge, including important deliverable characteristics

Avoid being too narrow or prescriptive

How are Partner Project Prompts developed?

Partner Companies work with ME310 Faculty, discuss questions, refine the statement
Statements are provided to ME310 Students at the Global Kick-Off

Starter Questions: 10 questions designed to start the conversation:

1. What do you consider to be your biggest market opportunity?
2. Where are your competitors making progress?
3. What problems are you having in developing product successes?
4. What don't you do well as a company that you'd like to do better?
5. Do you have any great ideas in your company that are going nowhere?
6. What products do you produce that might have application in other markets?
7. Do you have any interesting materials or ingredients looking for a product application?
8. What products have failed that should have been successful?
9. If you could introduce just one successful product next year, what would it be?
10. What project do you want to do?

Kenji Matsui, Ph.D.
ME310 corporate sponsor, AY2004–AY2010

> While traditional education considers the knowledge transfer to the student, students really need to understand how to grow, which skills are missing, and how to obtain those skills. This would establish their own goals and self-regulating study process.

My first visit to Stanford's Center for Design Research (CDR) was in December 2004. At that time, I was working at Panasonic's R&D office in San Jose, California. Larry Leifer raised many questions about our problems at his office. Immediately I was inspired by Larry's problem analysis process. In Japan, although new business creation was an urgent matter for most of the major electronics companies, innovation process was not formulated at that time. Many companies had tried 'corporate venturing' or 'corporate entrepreneurship'; however, most of these efforts were seed-oriented thinking. In general, corporate culture was the major deterrent to innovation. Leaders were rewarded by following rules.

After the first meeting with Larry, we started to implement the ME310 innovation process at our San Jose lab by kicking off the first project with Stanford students. Since then, Panasonic R&D joined the ME310 Industry Affiliates program and worked as a corporate partner several times with Stanford, as well as with ME310's global academic partners such as the Hasso Plattner Institut in Germany, Aalto Design Factory in Finland, etc.

We introduced the term 'design thinking' to our corporate R&D and product divisions at Panasonic. We received numerous and rather controversial responses. Looking back over those years, throughout all those challenges, I found that many of our lab members became design thinkers, and currently they have been actively working in various fields.

After I returned to Osaka, Japan, I gradually noticed that the design thinking process has to be in a school education program. The innovation process is not usually studied formally at school in Japan. Engineers who have just graduated have a body of knowledge, but they do not know engineering as a process. I have seen a lot of failure since I was a young engineer. If I had known about innovation as a process, I would have helped address some of those problems.

I then moved to the Osaka Institute of Technology (OIT) in 2011 as a Professor in the Department of Robotics. I started to create a few ME310-like programs with our global partners (from a week long to three months). OIT opened up several design-thinking related courses. Meanwhile, OIT decided to establish a new campus in the heart of Osaka as a multi-purpose building, which is 22 stories tall with 2 basement floors. I became one of the founding team members. I stole the 8th and 9th floors of the new campus to create a space modeled after Stanford's ME310 loft. In April 2017, when the campus opened, our Robotics & Design department was established, and 1,000 students began studying under the new curriculum.

The Osaka Chamber of Commerce and Industry (OCCI) soon came to us and discussed creating a joint open innovation space. In April 2018, OCCI and OIT established Xport in our loft space to encourage more academic and industry cross-collaboration. OIT faculty, students, and several partner companies are currently working together to solve their complex future challenges.

Overall, the ME310 course instills grit and radical change in our engineering education. I have been learning and running many projects every year. It is still not easy to produce innovative solutions; however, I am hoping to contribute to industries by sending over many newly minted design thinkers.

Currently Professor of Robotics at Osaka Institute of Technology

THE STANFORD DAILY

An Independent Newspaper

98th YEAR

VOLUME 197, NUMBER 39

THURSDAY, APRIL 19, 1990

Corporations help engineering students design solutions

By Ken Yew
Staff writer

With help from private corporations, Stanford engineering students are using their skills to solve real-world problems.

For example, the Mechanical Engineering Department's design division has worked with companies for years on design problems provided by corporations. For the past 15 years the department has run a program in which companies pay a membership fee to support technical courses at Stanford.

In exchange for solving their problems the companies pay for equipment and teaching assistants. In almost all cases "the sponsoring corporation retains ownership of the prototype," says Mechanical Engineering Prof. Larry Leifer. In some cases, if the students develop a patentable design, they have their names attached to the patent.

Leifer says the corporations give the department $500 to $20,000 for each course, depending on the scope of the budget agreed upon. The smaller number is typical of a 10-week undergraduate course.

Besides the money, the corporations provide "realistic problems, access to current industrial information and a strong motivating influence," Leifer says.

Leifer says the Mechanical Engineering Department depends on the companies to give students a feeling for how engineers work in the industrial sector. He and other professors say the lack of corporate involvement would reduce the intellectual curriculum of the department.

When Frederick Terman built the School of Engineering into a great institution, part of his original vision was to create ties between academia and industrial research. That vision was one of the primary reasons Stanford founded the Stanford Research Park.

History Prof. Joseph Corn says there

> 'The American university has always been very much a vehicle for larger social concerns and not necessarily configured for reflecting the desires of intellectuals.'
> — Joseph Corn

is nothing new about corporate involvement in universities. He mentions the example of the Burlington Railroad, which donated a locomotive engine for engineering students at Purdue University in the 19th century.

While some intellectuals may see corporate involvement as intrusive, Corn says, "The American university has always been very much a vehicle for larger social concerns and not necessarily configured for reflecting the desires of intellectuals."

Robert Anderson, a graduate mechanical engineering student in the three-quarter long Mechanical Engineering 210 sequence, is working with two other students on an "active aerodynamics" system for General Motors cars. The project involves creating a series of wings placed on the car that would move to enhance a car's braking and turning

Anderson says much of the technology involved in the project was new to them, and at first it was difficult to arrive at the detailed specifications for each of the wings.

Anderson says the course is "a big eye-opener" for students without any industrial experience. He said the course entrusts students with "the responsibility of handling a budget for the first time." Anderson's team had to deal with buying hardware for the prototype, buying computer time to do their analysis and even buying the services of outside analysts to do some of the heavier computation.

"The nature of project work is there are a lot of avenues where you have to make decisions, and there are turns that can lead you astray," Anderson says. "There's a large potential for wasted time."

Please see CLASSES, page 9

Gentlemen, build your engines

Classes

Continued from front page

He adds, "It takes a lot of legwork, but it's quite constructive and really expands one's mind."

Stanford computer science students got a chance to work on the state-of-the-art Next computer before it was introduced to private users. Paul Hegarty, a Next engineer, started a course on "object-oriented user interfaces" last autumn, which used the Next computer. Hegarty, a Stanford graduate, says he felt the topic was important for students to learn, and the Next computer "was a perfect platform to teach this."

Instead of the very rigid structured programming that characterizes other programming languages, the use of special computer functions, called "objects," obviates the need to control information flow.

The objects are functions that perform a task as well as all the tasks of lower-level functions. Whenever an object is called upon to perform a task, all the information that needs to be sent to other parts of the program will be transmitted automatically. Thus, the only thing a programmer needs to be concerned with is what the object is and what it does, and not how it fits in with other functions.

Hegarty says object-oriented programming will soon be the new standard for computer programming. "I can't see people sticking with C or Pascal, he says. The course benefits Next by having students familiar with the system because students who will go on to create software after graduation will use the Next's process. "It benefits us," Hegarty says, "to have more people who can do object-oriented interface systems."

While Next may benefit, the company contributed no equipment or money to the course, although it did provide the instructor. Next allowed Hegarty the time to work on the course as well as access to "0.9" versions of the Next computer, which are those machines released to programmers and companies before the Next was available to the general public. The machines are essentially the same in design, but they are released earlier.

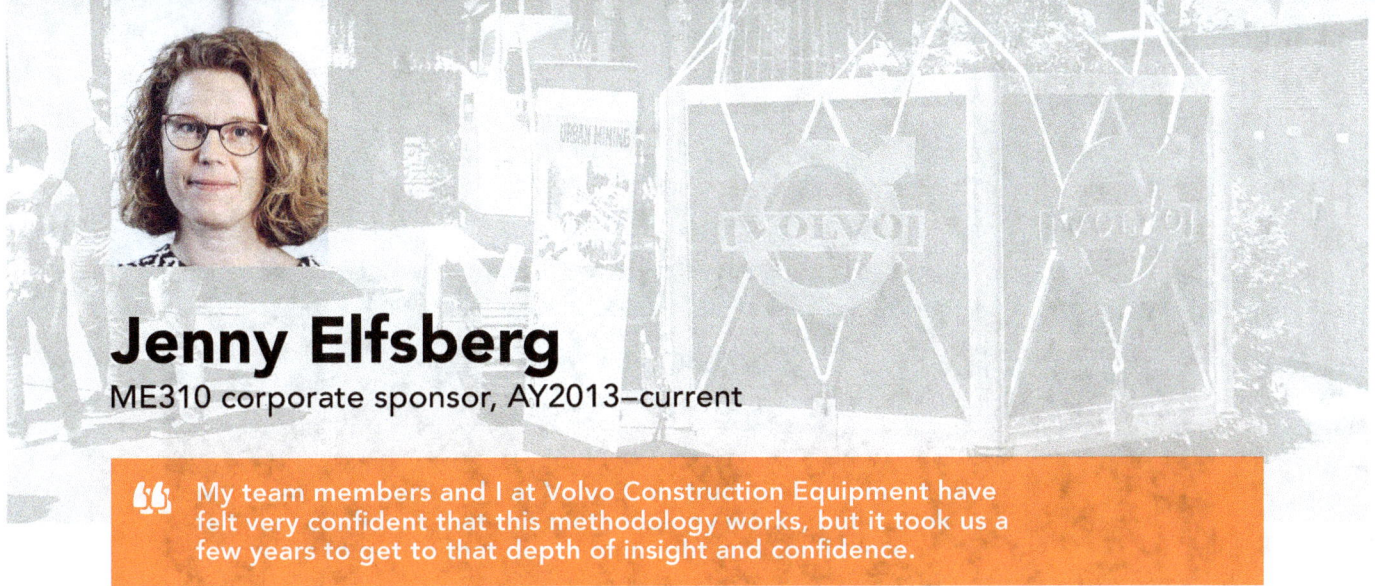

Jenny Elfsberg
ME310 corporate sponsor, AY2013–current

> My team members and I at Volvo Construction Equipment have felt very confident that this methodology works, but it took us a few years to get to that depth of insight and confidence.

To unlearn the traditional linear way of developing new concepts and shift into the iterative human-centered design paradigm isn't easy; you can't take a week-long course, and then have it embedded. Being a part of ME310 has helped tremendously. We learn both with and from the students at the same time they learn about us and from us. Not every year has ended with a 'triple wow' final concept to take further in Volvo, but every year has generated new customer insights that we can build upon and a deeper understanding of the design thinking way of working.

The combination of students at Stanford with students at the Blekinge Institute of Technology (BTH) in Sweden for each project adds important perspectives and value. Not only do the students cover different markets in their need-finding work, they also collaborate across cultures and time zones, and their different education systems also give valuable diversity.

As a result, we have learned how to build strong globally distributed teams and also learned to address the importance of diversity, frequent sharing, team trust, genuine care about team members, rapid prototyping iterations, an openness to 'kill your darling', the extreme importance of reflection time, and much more. No book, no training, and no management course could have given us the insights ME310 has given — but, of course, the learning curve has been much steeper due to the fact that I have taken online courses in parallel with my ME310 interactions.

Volvo has many extremely knowledgeable engineers with traditional technology domain knowledge in areas that have been our core for decades. Students today learn new technologies, such as additive manufacturing, artificial intelligence, connected systems (IoT), programming of Arduino, Raspberry Pi, Android, etc.

The new technologies enable students to provide new knowledge to companies like us, while our senior experts can give students the traditional knowledge. Also, the beginner's mind of a young student is tremendously useful during need-finding and the development of customer journey maps because the students are not biased towards looking for things related to our products. This enables more 'zoomed out' perspectives and potential innovations in product-service-system format rather than an incremental improvement of existing technical solutions.

Currently Director of Innovation Lab Hub US at Volvo Group

Teams

A critical part of the ME310 learning experience is working with and in teams. Coaches helps teams to understand what to do next, and much of the coaching occurs in small group meetings (called SGMs) that typically combine 2-3 teams. Large group meetings (or LGMs) refer to the full class session. In the early years, coaches were local Stanford alumni and industry experts, while coaches in recent years tend to be former students who have lived the design process. In the last three decades, the paper bike exercise has become an annual team-building ritual, exposing students to getting tangible, practicing a mini design challenge, and working as a team. — *Editor*

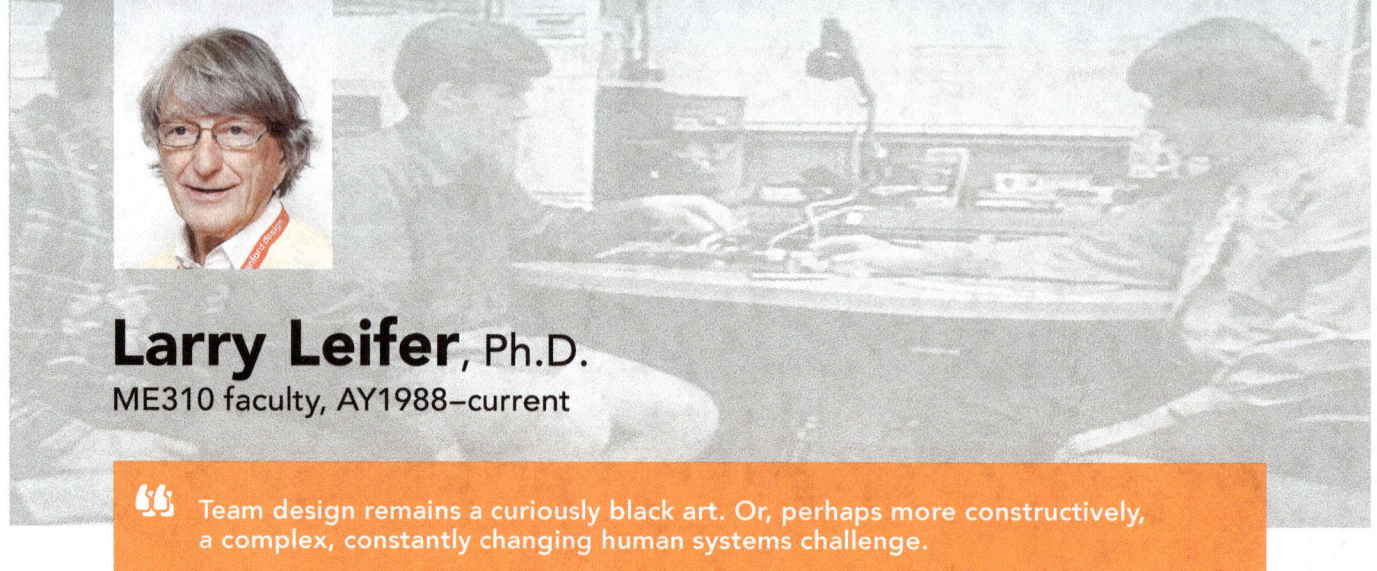

Larry Leifer, Ph.D.
ME310 faculty, AY1988–current

> Team design remains a curiously black art. Or, perhaps more constructively, a complex, constantly changing human systems challenge.

Several CDR dissertations have addressed the issue of teams. For example, Andrew Carrillo demonstrated that teams with high diversity outperformed teams with lower diversity in the long run (i.e., grades for Spring Quarter), but not much in the short run (i.e., grades for Autumn Quarter). His diversity variables were the familiar standards: age, expertise, gender, ethnicity, years of practice.

Greg Kress's dissertation revisited the issue a decade plus later. In a study of global teams, he looked at how 17 variables correlated with team performance as judged at the end of Spring quarter. The first 5 variables were the observable items listed above. The next 12 variables were Jungian personality preference archetypes. The presence of all variables correlated positively with performance — but weakly. Only one cognitive variable correlated strongly with performance, which was the team's collective score on empathy — extraverted feeling (Jungian terminology). We used the above factors rather successfully up through about 2015, and then, most projects had become human/machine interface challenges, and the student population was rapidly becoming dominated by non-USA citizens. Culture variables were moving into the foreground, and in some cases there were no Stanford undergraduates coming into the graduate student population that takes ME310. Everyone is a stranger to Stanford and even Silicon Valley thinking and doing.

We are struggling now with how to manage the art-of-team-formation given new human ingredients that are largely unknowable to us at the time teams need to be formed. This puts increased emphasis on having teams form themselves, e.g. take ownership of their choice of teammates.

Currently Professor of Mechanical Engineering at Stanford University

Mark Cutkosky, Ph.D.
ME310 coach, AY1990–AY2001; ME310 faculty, AY2002–current

Design has always been coaching-intensive. Each team has a different project. Therefore each team potentially needs different help at any given time. Coaching from alumni, now out in industry, is also important. They have a level of credibility for the teams about what really matters in the high-tech startup environment.

SGMs [*Small Group Meetings — editor*] are to track progress, give advice, etc. They also provide some structure because there are published expectations each week about what the SGMs should cover and what the teams should be prepared to show and explain. The teams sometimes complain that the SGMs can be stressful — but if they are, it is usually a sign that the team itself is not entirely clear on what it wants to do.

We have approached team formation and team dynamics in various ways over the years. For example, we have used some tools developed by Prof. Doug Wilde and others to help teams learn about themselves and what might constitute a good team. These tools often are most useful in that they provide a somewhat objective framework to organize students' thoughts and intuitions about what matters to them and what might be useful in forming a balanced team, independent of their personal feelings about people. We have also developed exercises to try to promote discovery of the preferences and working styles of other classmates before forming teams.

Currently Professor of Mechanical Engineering at Stanford University

ME310 DESIGN AXIOMS

1. DESIGN IS A SOCIAL PROCESS
2. ALL DESIGN IS REDESIGN
3. DESIGNERS NEED TO PRESERVE AMBIGUITY

Doug Wilde, Ph.D.
ME310 researcher, AY1991–AY1999

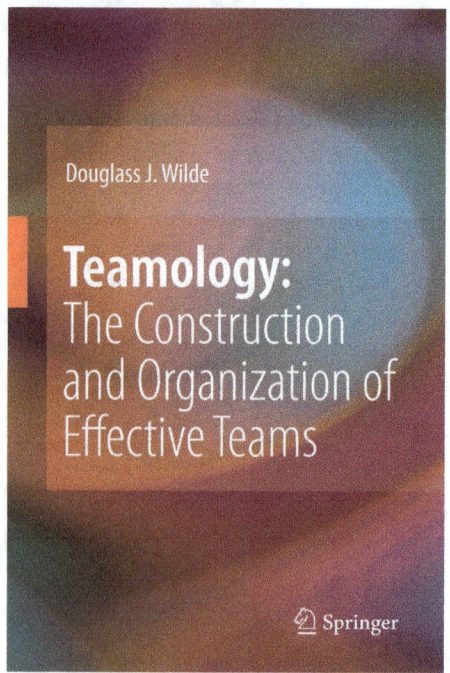

6.2.1 Creativity Workshop

In 1989, colleague James Adams introduced the MBTI [*Myers-Briggs Type Indicator — editor*] to a two-week Creativity Workshop held at Stanford's Design Division and supervised by Bernard Roth, Rolf Faste and the author. His point was that people are different and their differences should be taken into account when speaking of creativity, especially on teams.

Intrigued by this notion, the author went to the second edition of the MBTI Manual and learned of a quantitative 'Gough Creativity Index' (GCI) constructed empirically as a linear function of the four MBTI variables. The MBTI was then administered to the 1990 and 1991 workshops to discover that, with statistical significance, the workshop experience did improve the average GCI of the twenty-five or so participants, mostly professors of engineering design.

6.2.2 MBTI Prize Winners

Convinced then of the validity of the MBTI numbers, the author asked colleague Larry Leifer to have his graduate mechanical engineering design students be guided by the MBTI when forming their year-long project teams. No advice was offered them other than that they try to have different letters whenever possible.

The results were spectacular! The Stanford teams, only duets because of a shortage that year of students relative to projects, won ten Lincoln Foundation Design awards out of twelve offered nationally. Over the dozen years preceding, Stanford teams had never received more than four Lincoln awards, so Leifer then made the questionnaire a standard required feature of the course. And the author began the research described in this book as an informal retirement project.

6.2.3 Creativity Index for Trios and Quartets

…For the five years following the 1992 breakthrough just recounted, the teams were formed, not by the MBTI letters, but by distributing the highest GCI scores among the teams. Starting with 1991, over the first six years this technique doubled the fraction of teams, now trios and quartets, receiving Lincoln awards. In hindsight this procedure lent variety only to the information collection modes, entirely ignoring decision making.

6.2.4 Unintentional Relapse

During the author's absence from Stanford in 1995, team formation reverted to the very informal procedures of pre-questionnaire days in which people picked team-mates on proximity rather than personality. The results were depressingly predictable. The fraction of teams winning prizes dropped from one-half back to one-quarter while the number of team problems rose annoyingly. This was uncomfortable proof of the new ideas for making teams.

6.2.5 Full Modal Variety

Consequently Mark Cutkosky, who had just taken over the course from Leifer, reinstated the MBTI-style procedures, now using an abbreviated 20-item questionnaire that was computerized for easy student use by teaching assistant Mike McNelly. The McNelly code also incorporated the newfound principle of using all eight cognitive modes, thus seeking complete cognitive variety. That is, not only were the information Collection c-modes distributed, the Decision-making d-modes were also varied. The prize frequency immediately rose to three-quarters, a tripling of the base frequency of the preceding bad year, which matched that of the years before the new method. Although not scientific proof of the new cognitive variety approach, it was strong anecdotal evidence encouraging further exploration.

…In the year 2000 the course split into two as the old Design Division spun off a new Biomechanics Division with its own graduate project course. Lincoln prize frequencies were no longer useful measures of team effectiveness.

Currently Emeritus Professor of Mechanical Engineering at Stanford University

Michael McNelly
ME310 student, AY1996

I arrived at Stanford with many years of aerospace industry experience but had never had any formal education in design. ME310 was quite the eye opener for me, and the year after I took the class, I became a Research Assistant for it, working with Professor Doug Wilde. My Ph.D. involved studying the student teams that took the class, seeking the ideal team composition based upon psychological types. The basics of the team constructions was to use Myers-Briggs psychological typing to assemble teams with diverse psychological leanings which would (in theory) complement each other. The 'big idea' person works more effectively with the 'cross all the t's, dot all the i's' person, and vice versa. The raw data tying the ME310 team profiles to real-world results was invaluable and would not have been possible in a class structured in any other way.

Currently consulting

Gentlemen, build your engines

First-year masters students in Mechanical Engineering line up at the start of the Paper Bike Race, a project in their Mechanical Engineering 210A course.

Paper Bike Sample Challenges

Class year: **AY2007** Design and create a vehicle and mallet made of paper products capable of playing a game of Polo. The vehicle must contain a passenger with a mallet and a pusher.

Class year: **AY2009** Build a vehicle capable of traversing rough terrain that contains beach balls (the cargo) and a rider. Prepare your vehicle with water resistant features in anticipation for water soakers during the event.

Class year: **AY2012** Design and create vehicles that contain and player and a pusher to compete in a game of dodgeball against all other design teams.

Class year: **AY2013** Based on the popular child's game "Hungry Hungry Hippos," design and build a vehicle capable of carrying a rider and beach balls that will be collected in the competition.

Class year: **AY2014** Create a vehicle to compete in teams with an objective to defend and collect bananas. Each vehicle should be created with two positions in mind: vehicle pusher/puller and banana picker.

Class year: **AY2015** Design and build a chariot that will be raced against other chariots on a track that includes obstacles and rough terrain.

Class year: **AY2016** Design, build, and test a human/machine team that captures Pokémon in Pokémon Go.

Class year: **AY2017** The challenge lies in designing and building a paper bike that can handle a variety of challenging terrain, from potholes and fallen branches to roadways doused in water.

Mark Cutkosky, Ph.D.
ME310 coach, AY1990–AY2001; ME310 faculty, AY2002–current

My recollection is that the paper bike exercise was introduced by Larry Leifer shortly after he took over the course in the 1990s. He felt the need to have a warm-up exercise that would give everybody a shared mini-design experience with the following elements: attention to ergonomics, material and manufacturing constraints and knowledge, rapid prototyping, and the need to document the design and design process. There is a paper by Bernie Roth and Rolf Faste about design projects in classes, which suggests that the projects should be different every year so that nobody knows a priori what the 'right' solution is. For paper bikes, we therefore pose a different challenge each year. However, we keep the material constraint, which encourages teams to look at previous solutions and to consult with alumni about fabrication techniques and materials sources.

Currently Professor of Mechanical Engineering at Stanford University

Zoom

Master's student Vincent Chiu tests a paper bicycle yesterday in the Quad. Three-person teams in the Mechanical Engineering 210 course had just over two weeks to develop the vehicles, using only paper and cardboard.

Lunnon Miles — Daily

Peddling papers

Matthew Lawrence — Daily

Graduate student Ted Acworth pedals his team's paper bicycle to victory over his classmates in Mechanical Engineering 210. Acworth and his teammates, graduate students Mike Graham and Rod Zylztra, broke the all time record for paper bicycle competitions.

Larry Leifer, Ph.D.
ME310 faculty, AY1988–current

I am not sure what motivated me beyond wanting a 'team warm-up activity', kind of like a pre-season game in the sports metaphor, including the fact that the outcome does not affect the grade. And as an unfamiliar design challenge, no one can pretend to be an expert. The duration is short to encourage moving, building and testing.

I like that the human/user is almost self evident. Year after year, teams think the bike rider is the user, and only after they assemble and use the vehicle in a practice game might they discover that the pusher/puller is actually the most critical user. This distinction is very important going forward into the industry-sponsored project as there are always many 'stakeholder' candidates of the critical user role.

The paper bike tradition is not a ritual in the sense of 'worthless but we do it'. It is a critical pedagogic element. This is emphasized when we demand a 'final report = what did you do?; why did you do it?; and what did you learn from it?' This design documentation requirement with its emphasis on the 'design rationale' is virtually unique in problem-based learning (PBL).

There are lots of 'final reports' in PBL caps courses, but they focus on documenting what was built, not the WHY WHY of each prototype. The ME310 paper bike documentation also introduces the most important deliverable of the course, that final report in June that must once again document = 'what did you do?; why did you do it?; and what did you learn from it?'

Currently Professor of Mechanical Engineering at Stanford University

David Radcliffe, Ph.D.
ME310 faculty, AY1991

Bernie Roth added several degrees of difficulty to the traditional 'paper bike' project by including a circumnavigation of the pond next to the former Terman building as part of the race circuit. Many soggy bikes did not survive this most severe of tests!

Currently Epistemology Professor Emeritus of Engineering Education at Purdue University

David Cannon, Ph.D.
ME310 student, AY1986; ME310 coach, AY1990, AY1992–AY1995

One of the first things that comes to mind when the subject of ME310 comes up is the paper bike race. The paper bike race is an interesting story to everyone — it's a simple race, after all, and everybody gets races. Further, it is run in vehicles made out of unusual materials, designed and built in two weeks, so that things regularly fall apart along the way.

The bike race was started by Larry Leifer (and maybe Mark Cutkosky) in the late 1980s or early '90s, shortly after Larry first got involved in the course. I recall talking with Larry in his office overlooking the Terman pond one day about some other issue, and he floated the idea of a paper bike race. I'm sure he'd been thinking about it for a while.

His thinking was clear: the bicycle is such a familiar and accessible thing for everyone, plus a nice example of the good qualities of engineering, that it's often taken for granted. And then you grab the students' attention — and that of an audience — by proposing that the bikes can be built out of something which, at first blush, sounds absurd: paper. Further, you're going to challenge the students, fresh into their master's degrees — for many just after they've entered a new and intimidating environment — to team up, design, build, and race such a thing in a short time.

You let up just a little: in fact, the 'bicycle' could be any human-propelled vehicle with wheels, not just a two-wheeler, and you might allow a little non-paper material, though teams would be penalized for it, say by weight. Larry made it part of the class right away, and I think it's been one of the first things to happen regularly in the class ever since.

Sometimes the paper bike race feels a little cruelly voyeuristic to watch. All these vehicles, made mostly of carpet rolls and heavy cardboard laminations precariously stuck together with tape, glue, and lashings, start off propelled by hopeful, nervous, exhausted students. Most of these students have only been at Stanford for a month, and most of them have lost a lot of sleep in the previous few nights trying to make their contraption operate like they had imagined it to do.

After the race starts, with few exceptions, these bikes begin to distort, sag, wobble, and creak. A mixture of determination and panic appears on the students' faces. They push forward, trying to figure out how to adjust, to hold things together, to compete, or they just hope they can go fast enough to get to the finish line before something collapses. It's exciting and comical to see, and at the same time, anyone who's taken on such a mad effort feels some painful empathy for the students' lot.

Subsequently, the students get to see each other under pressure. This can bring out the worst and best in others and in oneself. After the race, they get to reevaluate how they behaved themselves and how others acted. This informs how they team up for their main projects and how they learn to work better. In retrospect, the comic absurdity of the race also gives many a chance to take their work a little less seriously and learn: we got through the race, didn't do as well as we're used to, and we're still kicking. It exposes people to the benefits and challenges of teamwork. This is one of the core tenets of the class: that your technical education can be valuable, but this value will be very much blunted unless you can work well with others.

Currently Postdoctoral Researcher at NASA Langley Research Center

Kenji Matsui, Ph.D.
ME310 corporate sponsor, AY2004–AY2010

I was inspired by Stanford's ME310 Paper Bike exercise, so several years ago, I created a variation for my design students in Japan using cardboard and ducks. We didn't have the same large space as the ME310 loft, so I wanted a team exercise that could be done in the same spirit but in less physical space. It works very well at OIT.

Currently Professor of Robotics at Osaka Institute of Technology

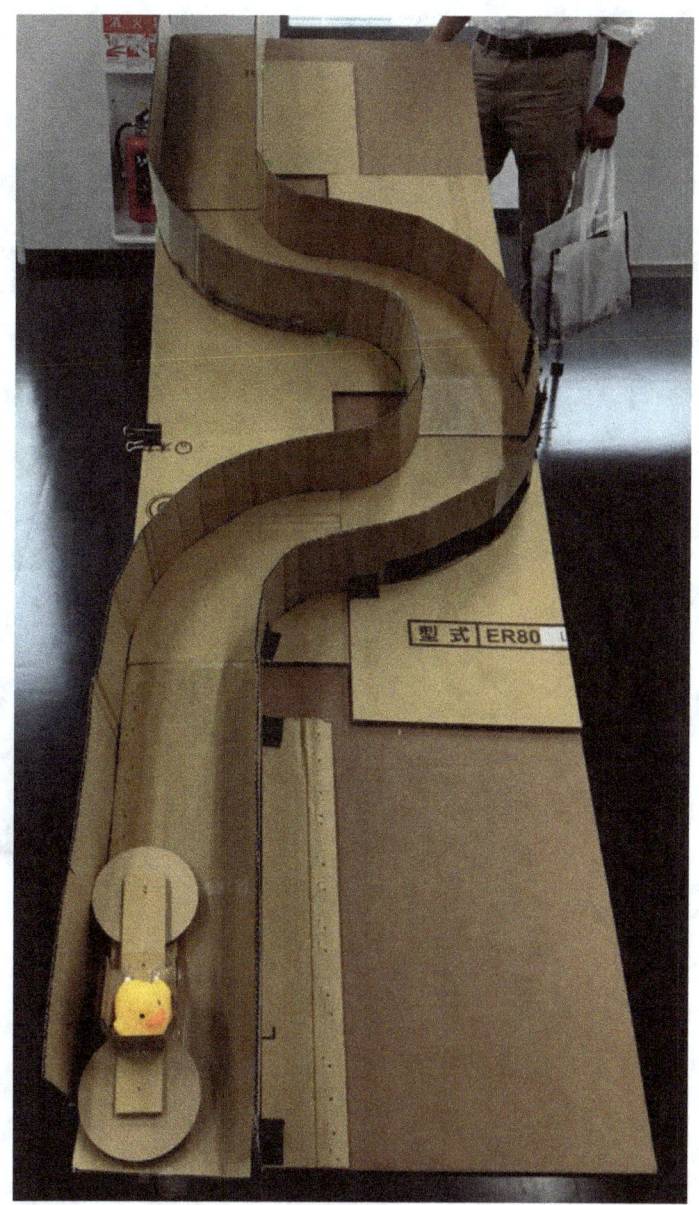

```
Warm Up Exercise:
Duck Slide Challenge


- Team-based exercise using a 3 meter long
  slide

- Each team must carry a small, medium, or
  large size duck on your vehicle.

- The score is depend on the duck size and
  the time.

- Only cardboard and tape are allowed to
  use.

- Taping the duck to the vehicle is not
  allowed. Duck must be free from the
  vehicle.

- Each team can try three times.

- Very unique designs or structured
  vehicles will be rewarded.

- You can test your vehicle before the
  competition and improve it many times.
```

Loft

Unlike most college courses, which reserve classroom space as needed, ME310 has a dedicated room for students to use throughout the academic year. This physical space is important for two reasons. First, students see artifacts from prior years surrounding them that reinforce their learning. Second, they soon adopt the room, dubbed the "ME310 loft", for other purposes, such as an extra study hall or break room outside their dorms, which encourages cross-talk and knowledge spillover across teams. The teaching team also aims to foster a sense of community in the ME310 loft via informal events. In recent years, teams rotate hosting a weekly class dinner called SUDS (Slightly Unorganized Design Session, plus beer pun). — *Editor*

Jim Adams, Ph.D.
ME310 faculty, AY1967–AY1970

I was involved in the original design loft. When I joined the faculty, I was straight out of NASA's Jet Propulsion Lab, but I had studied industrial design in UCLA's Art Department and done my graduate engineering work at Stanford before then. Like architecture and other established design programs, the UCLA program had a large studio, in which the students spent a large amount of time.

I was brought to Stanford partly because I had a mixed background in engineering and art and because Bob McKim needed help not only in teaching undergraduate courses, but also wanted to start a Stanford graduate program in product design. But they had no studio.

Stanford's High Temperature Gas Dynamics group had a lot of money and status and was trying to take over as much space as possible in the old shop complex. Clearly a studio was needed, and there was a loft over the foundry, which we happily took over and 'improved'. As is usually the case with self-built facilities, we all loved it; the only downside being that we had to vacate it when classes were pouring in the foundry, because toxic gas tends to rise.

The Product Design program was later to move to its present location on campus, because more civilized space became available, but the students continued to call their space the 'loft'. I guess that has now become a sort of tradition in the ME310 design program.

Currently Emeritus Professor of Mechanical Engineering at Stanford University

Bernie Roth, Ph.D.
ME310 faculty, fall 1972, AY1991

In 1972, the Design Division occupied the top floor of the Engineering corner of the Main Quad. We had two large design studio type classrooms that were used for teaching drafting and other undergraduate design courses, so space had to be found elsewhere. A permanent space was found for the students' project work in building 570, which at the time also contained the student shop. This space became the home for the ME310 course. Interestingly there was a loft adjacent to this space. The loft was used for the Product Design Masters students, who had to enter it by climbing a ladder. Their space was a true loft, not one in name only.

Currently Professor of Mechanical Engineering at Stanford University

Mark Cutkosky, Ph.D.
ME310 coach, AY1990–AY2001; faculty, AY2002–current

The physical space is very important. It is one of the first things that impresses visitors when they come to learn about the class and about project-based engineering education in general.

It is intentionally a bit like a 'low rent' version of a Bay Area design consultancy. And it is also a bit like an artist's studio (a bottega in the Italian tradition) with plenty of quick prototyping tools and materials on hand. The idea is to make the cost very low for rapidly assembling something to explore an idea. It also helps to have a shared space to foster communication among the teams and a space in which they can leave works in process without fear that they will be cleaned up or carted away.

Currently Professor of Mechanical Engineering at Stanford University

Micah Lande, Ph.D.
ME310 student, AY2005; teaching assistant, AY2006–AY2007

Curiously, there were never quite enough red chairs in the loft for everyone. I like to think that it was a purposeful and planned out thing. Maybe another research project intended to better recognize the patterns of work as teams would ready for their SGMs [*Small Group Meetings — editor*] across the room over Tuesday and Thursday afternoon. Or to get people to mix together at SUDS [*Slightly Unorganized Design Session — editor*] over food and drink Thursday evening. ME310 itself is a social activity.

Currently Assistant Professor and E.R. Stensaas Chair for Engineering Education at South Dakota School of Mines and Technology

SUDS in the loft

Showcase

In the early years, students presented final prototypes to sponsoring companies at year-end meetings. These presentations gradually evolved into a year-end event known as "Demo Days", which then became part of the Design Affiliates Symposium (or Conference) through the 1990s. Then through the 2000s and 2010s, these presentations have anchored a Stanford Mechanical Engineering departmental event called "Design EXPErience", called EXPE for short. This day-long showcase is open to the public and features ME310 presentations in the morning and live demos — trade show style — of the team prototypes in the afternoon. This showcase finale offers a way for companies to see ideas across all projects and partners. — *Editor*

Larry Leifer, Ph.D.
ME310 faculty, AY1988–current

It is possible that the evolution of our class 'Mission Statements' is another data source for team reflection. Note that I borrowed missions from Chris Gerdes because a mission is open-ended, whereas calling something an assignment pretty much demands the 'right answer'. This is another one of those ME310 inventions that incoming students do not understand and keep asking us 'what's the assignment, really?'.

Also, I like Mark [Cutkosky]'s testimonial that seeing ME310 project outcomes at EXPE brought him to Stanford. Quotable! EXPE is that final phase of the football metaphor when you actually have to show up with something and present it to strangers, not just your instructors and TAs [*Teaching Assistants — editor*] who already know the story. It is also a chance to celebrate together. And, after all of the isolated teamwork, we all come together for one event instead of 10 separate events or grades.

Currently Professor of Mechanical Engineering at Stanford University

Focus on industrial design
VW partners with Stanford

By BOB BOREK
CONTRIBUTING WRITER

The recent partnership between Stanford and Volkswagen Automotive University, an institution of post-graduate education run by the corporation, could yield both advanced driving technology and greater opportunities for doctoral students to gain research experience with industry professionals.

The collaboration — outlined in an agreement signed on May 4 by Larry Leifer, director of the Stanford Center of Design Research; Peter Hartz, a member of the Board of Management of Volkswagen; and Walther Zimmerli, president of Volkswagen Automotive University — is focused on the area of industrial design.

The contract stipulates that an Automotive University employee spend a year working and researching industrial design at Stanford. Additionally, two Stanford professors will give lectures and courses at the Automotive University. Volkswagen's electronic research lab in Palo Alto will also participate in the project.

"The Stanford Design community brings fresh ways of thinking, an emphasis on innovation and design-thinking," said Leifer, a mechanical engineering professor at Stanford.

"I think the partnership between Stanford and Volkswagen Auto-Uni is a fair trade-off," said Auto-Uni Prof. Hans Ulrich Gumbrecht. "Auto-Uni hopes to profit from Stanford's academic expertise and prestige as an institution — it wants to learn. Stanford, I assume, hopes to develop interesting collaboration in high-tech with Volkswagen, through the university."

Gumbrecht himself is a link between Stanford and Volkswagen as he is a professor in Stanford's Comparative Literature Department as well as a member of the scientific board and the academic advisory board at Volkswagen Auto-Uni.

Cooperation between academics and auto-design moguls is nothing new for Stanford University. For instance, the Mechanical Engineering Department's Engine Lab and contemporary nanotechnology research projects are closely related

Please see VW, page 2

VW
Continued from front page

to automotive fuel cells.

"In the long run we expect to link Stanford to all 20 Auto-Uni remote sites," Leifer said. "In time, the Stanford Center for Professional Development will probably host these courses."

Officials at Stanford and Volkswagen Auto-Uni said they hope to "develop an advanced cockpit simulator with vehicle dynamics simulation to explore the human-machine-interaction issues for driver-safety-assistance," he said.

"That includes augmented driving sensation based on GPS-aware road information and accommodations for an aging driver population that now includes people over 75 as the fastest growing segment of the driving population," Leifer added.

The shift in the driving demographic will play a central role in the research conducted by Stanford and Volkswagen Auto-Uni. Because older and younger people will be expected to rapidly adapt to new technology, innovations must be user-friendly so that one can operate them almost intuitively.

Leifer made it clear that the collaboration should not be interpreted as Volkswagen outsourcing its design work to Stanford students and researchers. Rather, Stanford will help strengthen the company's design process by identifying areas for improvement.

"Volkswagen is not outsourcing their design at all," he said. "They are outsourcing the redesign of their design methodology because it can not readily be done internally."

Leifer said that Volkswagen tends to be very "user-centered" in their thinking, which allows for greater creativity.

"The joint venture is a very healthy approach to broadening the diversity factor in corporate thinking and in our own students' academic expertise," he added.

Sample Projects 1970s–80s

Class year: AY1977
Project title: Redesign of the San Francisco Cable Car Grip
Corporate sponsor: San Francisco Municipal Railway

The San Francisco cable car system had changed little in the last 100 years, so a NASA Ames Research Center study recommended improving its grip. The Stanford team proposed and tested a design that utilized wheels and clutch components instead of the soft steel dies in the present system. Their solution met several key design requirements, including passenger safety, cost savings, and supporting a cable car weighing up to 25,000 pounds.

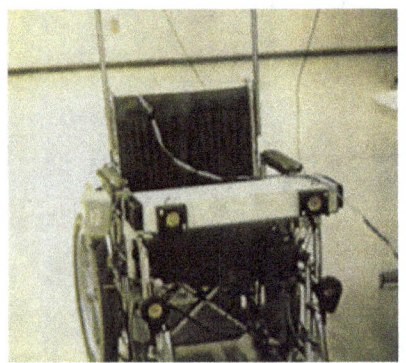

Class year: AY1979
Project title: Head Control / Smart Wheelchair
Corporate sponsors: Veterans Admin. Hospital, Stanford Children's Hospital

The sponsors asked for an innovative control and guidance system for an electric motorized vehicle used by severely handicapped persons, specifically quadriplegics and Cerebral Palsy victims. Unlike commercially-available electric wheelchairs, the design had to move with minimum user input. The team used voice recognition software combined with ten Polaroid ultrasonic range-finding sensors to modify and reprogram an existing smart wheelchair.

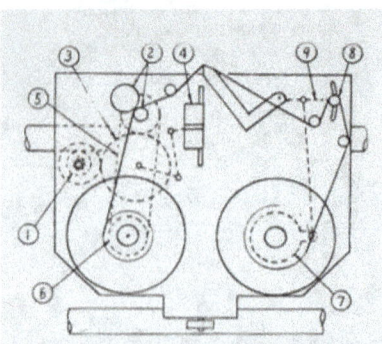

Class year: AY1982
Project title: A Speed Controlled Film Handling Device
Corporate sponsor: IBM

IBM wanted a device that would transport plastic film without affecting film speed while maintaining proper tension. Unlike other conventional film handling devices, the students built a purely mechanical mechanism that used a frictional rack and pinion for power generation, a cam-switched idler-type transmission, a capstan film drive, and a variable torque brake for supply side film tension control. Testing confirmed design concept feasibility.

Sample Projects 1980s

Class year: AY1984
Project title: Robotic Collision Avoidance System
Corporate sponsor: FMC Corporation

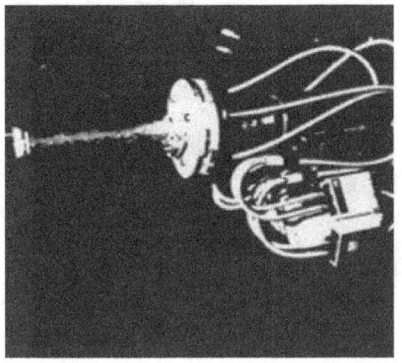

Industrial manufacturer FMC Corporation asked the students to develop a collision avoidance system for its factory robots to use in welding, part inspection, and material handling tasks. The students designed a mechanical apparatus to attach the welding tools and sensors to a robot, an electronic circuit to detect collisions and trigger an emergency stop, and a RAIL-based software routine to control the system and make decisions.

Class year: AY1985
Project title: An Intravenous Flow Control Pump
Corporate sponsor: Travenol Laboratories

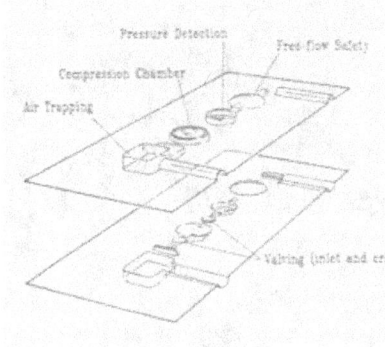

The challenge from Travenol was to develop a product concept that was more accurate than the pinch roller clamp for controlling the medication flow rate in a medical intravenous bag (IV bag). The students focused on the pump cassette design, using a stepping motor as the primary electromechanical device. Their design resulted in a two-piece cassette, vacuum formed from sheets of polymer film and heat sealed together.

Class year: AY1989
Project title: Electronics Ceramic Breaking
Corporate sponsor: Ford Motor Company

Ford wanted to automate its ceramic breaking operation, then done manually, at their Pennsylvania electronics plant. A literature review revealed that it was difficult to induce a breaking moment without damaging electronic components. The students designed a low-cost, automated ceramic breaking prototype, consisting of a padded wheel suspended on a conveyor belt. Ford planned to implement it in production immediately.

Sample Projects 1990s

Class year: AY1990
Project title: Single Passenger Commuter Vehicle Cockpit
Corporate sponsor: BMW (Bavarian Motor Works)

BMW wished to develop a means of seating a wide range of car driver sizes, assuming a fixed eye point with conventional steering and pedal controls in their cars. The student team discovered that a fixed eye point requires multiple adjustments including seat height, steering column, foot pedal, and auxiliary control locations, so their prototype implemented these adjustments in a full-scale seating buck to correctly align the eyepoint of the driver.

Class year: AY1993
Project title: Dairy Capping Equipment
Corporate sponsor: Cap Snap Co.

Cap Snap made 4+ billion tamper-evident caps annually for the dairy and water industry. The company asked the students to develop a parts feeding device that was more efficient than the present equipment and modular in design for easy assembly and installation. The team explored two solutions: a vertical spinner modified from an existing commercial product and a modular chute that met the capping speed requirement of 300 caps per minute.

Class year: AY1996
Project title: A Faying Surface Area Gap Measurement Apparatus
Corporate sponsor: Boeing Commercial Airplane Group

Boeing wanted to change their manual shim fabrication process to an automated system that could measure a gap, create a shim from this measurement, and record this data to track manufacturing history and perform a statistical process control analysis. The students built a prototype using the Gapman by Capacitec and gap measurement locator.

Sample Projects 2000s–10s

Class year: AY2006
Project title: Artificial Sense of Direction for Pedestrians
Corporate sponsor: Panasonic
Academic partner: University of Tokyo, Japan

Panasonic asked the joint team from Stanford and the University of Tokyo to develop a wearable navigation tool aimed at pedestrians. The team decided to address the problem of user distraction and give users an infallible sense of direction with minimal intervention. Their design used a central processing unit (as a web-enabled mobile phone) connected to a wrist-mounted three-axis compass with vibration feedback and multi-colored LED lights.

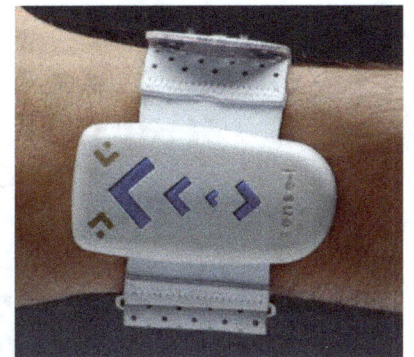

Class year: AY2011
Project title: Modernizing the Paper Notebook for the Digital Age
Corporate sponsor: SAP
Academic partner: University of Science and Technology of China, China

Despite the growth of digital tablets, no device had yet taken a significant portion of the market, as many manual writing processes are used. A joint team of Stanford and USTC students designed a digital notetaking device that met the extreme needs of field researchers. Their design combined a Wacom electromagnetic resonance screen with a low-gloss textured surface, a notebook interface, and intelligent character recognition software.

Class year: AY2013
Project title: CareSquare: Clinic-in-a-backpack
Corporate sponsor: United Nations Children's Fund (UNICEF)
Academic partner: Aalto University, Finland

In Nigeria, the rate of child mortality remains very high due to the lack of medical access and intense commute for women. Stanford and Aalto students created a portable healthcare station for the healthcare worker, designed to impact the three largest factors of childhood mortality: low vaccination rates, malaria, and diarrhea. UNICEF planned an independent backpack project in the near future, using this student project as input.

Next stop: Mars

Masters student Wayne Fu's Mechanical Engineering 210 project makes for the sky above the bed of Lake Lag yesterday.

Sam Mankiewicz — Daily

Global

Nearly every year, the ME310 teaching team revises the class curriculum and format to better support learning goals. By 2005, Professor Larry Leifer realized that ME310 students should experience design innovation as a distributed team process that mirrors industry practice. He reached out to trusted partners in his network, partnering Stanford ME310 student teams with student teams at other universities worldwide. That "team-of-teams" collaboration gradually became a movement known as SUGAR (temporarily a mock acronym that stood for the Stanford University Global Alliance for Redesign), whose members have adopted and grown the ME310 model around the globe. — *Editor*

Larry Leifer, Ph.D.
ME310 faculty, AY1988–current

At the time that I was advocating turning ME310 into a global collaboration in the mid-2000s, I was also involved in research at CDR [*Stanford Center for Design Research — editor*] related to engineering design knowledge capture studies. We had several international research partners, and they became our earliest ME310-Global academic partners. Rolf Lenshow from NTNU (Norwegian University of Science and Technology) was one of them, and we broke ground using video conferencing technology that typically cost $50k–75k. Skype and Facetime today have made distant collaboration cheaper, not better. In contrast, CDR's designXlab research studied what really made team dynamics and performance work. For example, Andrew Milne took his study of Terry Winograd's 'design room' to form the company Tidebreak.

Mark Cutkosky often remarks that our global 'team-of-teams' (as we learned to refer to our network well before Stanley McCrystal's book) was not obviously leading to better needfinding or design-implementations, BUT IT WAS leading to better design documentation with a working hypothesis that the two teams needed to communicate better to work together. Ask Mark.

There was also the growing fact that more and more products, services, and businesses were global, and that for an ME310 graduate to be ready to work globally 'out of the box', he or she would need to have global experiences while still in ME310 — our own 'flight emulator'. Many alumni have testified to the value of that experience.

Currently Professor of Mechanical Engineering at Stanford University

Bernhard Schindlholzer, Ph.D.
ME310 global partner, AY2006–AY2008

> In the early stages, there was a lot of skepticism from HSG administration, but the enthusiasm from students — some stating that this was the best course they ever had — helped. Of course, acquiring CHF 360k from industry partners also helped!

'Why should U.S.-based engineering students team up with Swiss-based business students in a joint course to solve problems for industry partners? Isn't that destined to fail from the start?' Questions like this have been omnipresent in the early stages of the ME310 collaboration between Stanford and the Institute of Information Management at the University of St. Gallen (HSG). Despite the uncertainty about the potential of such a collaboration on both sides, the course was off to a start in autumn 2006, led by Philipp Skogstad who was the initial driver to bring ME310 to St. Gallen.

In the early phases, even the physical space requirements were questioned: why does a course at a business school need a special setup that allows students to brainstorm in an open environment, put post-its on a wall, and build prototypes? Ten years later, such environments cannot just be found on campuses all over the world but also increasingly in corporations aiming to adapt a more innovative and agile way of work.

The enthusiastic feedback from HSG students about the first course made it clear that this new didactic approach needed to continue at HSG. Under the leadership from Axel Hochstein and Walter Brenner, the scope was expanded and more collaborations with industry partners were established. Falk Uebernickel took the course to another level and expanded into executive education and training, in addition to an even further expansion of industry partnerships in the core ME310 course.

One unique aspect of ME310 is the approach to let students learn and experience firsthand the challenges of working across different domains, cultures, and time zones. The initial reaction is often frustration and a feeling of being overwhelmed with the complexity of the course. Yet in these moments, the unique teaching methodology developed in ME310 helped the students to take major steps forward in their understanding of engineering design, business design, and successful collaboration for innovation.

What started as a teaching experiment has over time turned into a critical course in the curriculum of business students at the University of St. Gallen. A central factor for this development was Larry Leifer's involvement and leadership that enabled the initial collaboration and paved the way for the evolution of the ME310 design methodology in a business environment. A fascinating observation was Larry's engagement that inspired students, faculty and business partners equally to explore innovation not just as a course but as a way of life.

Reflecting on his leadership style also shows that Larry Leifer practices what he preaches. In one of the first workshops with a ME310 partner in Switzerland, the CEO of a major Swiss company asked Larry: 'What's the secret to get your company to be more innovative?'

Larry's response was straightforward: 'It's easy. 3 characters. You need to L-E-T innovation happen.'

And this is also how ME310 was able to establish and evolve itself not just in St. Gallen but all over the world: Larry Leifer inspires people and then lets innovation happen.

Currently Product Manager at Google

Reinhold Steinbeck
ME310 liaison for Latin America, AY2007–current

> ME310 hadn't had a global academic partner in South America before 2007. As a matter of fact, until then all of ME310's academic partners had come from the global north.

'Why do you want to take Stanford students to Colombia?' was the first question I was asked when I approached the Office of Risk Management at Stanford University. That was a very appropriate question, one I was ready for, as the perception of Colombia still very much involved drug-related violence. But when I had first reached out to the Pontificia Universidad Javeriana (PUJ) in Cali in 2007, the reality of the Colombian situation was already changing. And how could one not be intrigued by a government PR campaign with the slogan 'Colombia Is Passion'?

At the time, I was directing the Stanford University International Outreach Program, also known as IOP. IOP was an academic start-up program that supported partnerships between Stanford and universities in Africa, Asia, and South America. Its main objective was to connect Stanford's most innovative teaching programs with universities in the global south. IOP already supported collaborations around mobile environmental science courses with universities in Africa and around teacher education with the Catholic University of Chile. Since I'd worked with Larry Leifer at the Stanford Learning Lab in the mid-1990s, I was very familiar with ME310 and determined to expand this innovative teaching program to the global south.

Krista Donaldson, a research associate with the Stanford Center for Design Research (CDR), put me in touch with Maria Fernanda Camacho, who was already teaching a product design course at PUJ in Cali. Things happened very quickly after that.

After first making contact in March 2007, by the end of July we were welcoming PUJ as an ME310 academic partner for the 2007-08 academic year. PUJ has been a reliable and consistent academic partner for ME310 ever since, and both ME310 as well as the SUGAR Network are now an integrated part of the university.

So what were some of the key factors that allowed us to bring a new academic partner from the global south to the ME310 program in such a short period of time?

1. Partner development: IOP, as part of Stanford's International Initiative, was able to put the university's institutional weight behind the development of this new partnership. IOP acted as the main coordinator throughout the early phase; it also facilitated the negotiations with Stanford's Office of Risk Management.

2. Bottom-up interest and top-down support: With Maria Fernanda as a local champion experienced in human-centered design and with strong support

from the Dean of the School of Engineering as well as from the vice rector of the university, PUJ was fully behind a partnership with ME310.

3. Resources: Through IOP, I was able to support Maria's initial visit to Stanford to meet the ME310 teaching team. IOP also organized and supported a follow-up site visit in which Larry and Philipp Skogstad, associate director of CDR, joined me for three days at PUJ in Cali. The site visit provided Larry and Philipp with the opportunity to meet with students, professors, and PUJ's leadership and to check out the university's infrastructure, address any safety concerns, and build crucial relationships.

4. Safety first: IOP, ME310, and the team from PUJ worked closely with Stanford's Office of Risk Management to put in place a solid protocol for guaranteeing the safety of Stanford students when visiting Colombia. While Stanford recommended that students not travel to Colombia, it did not prohibit graduate students from doing so. The protocol from the ME310 teaching team and the leadership team at PUJ included pre-departure briefings to inform students of the risks associated with traveling to Colombia and Cali; requirements for local transportation and on-campus accommodation; communication with the U.S. Embassy in Colombia; and outlining to Colombian students their responsibilities in hosting their visitors from Stanford.

5. Small private institution: PUJ Cali is the smaller satellite campus of PUJ Bogotá, a private Jesuit university. Decisions can be made faster there, and resources are available. For example, the university was able to create a dedicated 'ME310 loft space' quickly. It also agreed to delegate some of the financial administration and responsibility of the ME310 projects to student teams, something that had been almost unheard of before.

6. Last, but not least, passion: PUJ put in place a rigorous selection process for identifying the students who were to participate in the ME310 program. From the very beginning, those chosen for the program were highly qualified and motivated, certainly living up to the slogan 'Colombia Is Passion'.

I call this effort of ME310 going to South America as dancing with ambiguity — and adding some hot salsa steps to it. 'Dancing with ambiguity' has been a trademark phrase of Larry Leifer that describes the need to not only let change happen in an innovation process, but also to promote it. With regard to 'hot salsa', Cali is known as the capital of salsa dancing in South America. As an avid salsa dancer, I might argue that dancing is also good for innovation and creativity, as it encourages you, and maybe even forces you, to let go of fear and embrace ambiguity.

Currently Managing Director of IntoActions

Maria Camacho, Ph.D.
ME310 global partner, AY2007–AY2010, AY2013

> In those seven years, Javeriana was central in the creation and consolidation of the SUGAR Network, collaborating in eight projects with Aalto University, UNAM, UniMore and St. Gallen University.

A series of rather amusing events led Pontificia Universidad Javeriana in Cali, Colombia, to be a long-term academic partner of ME310. In March 2007, I was having lunch with Larry at the Faculty Club at Stanford to discuss the possibility of Javeriana joining ME310. Larry Leifer was keen to engage a university from a developing country, and Stanford's international relations area had funded my trip, in time to witness the winter presentations. Then at lunch Larry said something like, 'I don't think this can happen. I don't know you, it's too risky. I've always worked in ME310 with people and institutions I know.' My face went blank. He kept saying it was not going to happen. We had been joined by ME310's then executive director Philipp Skogstad and Reinhold Steinbeck from Stanford International Relations, who were convinced Javeriana and I were the right partner; they were trying hard for Larry to change his mind. But he was quite set in his argument. So I said to him: 'Come and visit us. You say you don't know us; well, come and get to know us'. And so he went. At the end of his trip, he said: 'Javeriana is a partner worth having; it is a university of excellence'.

In September 2007, we started collaborating on two projects, and we never looked back. In my time at Javeriana until 2014, Stanford and Javeriana collaborated on 10 projects with companies from the U.S., Japan, Spain, Peru and Colombia.

In 2013, I secured a project with Colombian multinational Totto for an ME310 collaboration with Stanford. Soon after, I got a Ph.D. fellowship at Swinburne University of Technology in Australia. I would have to leave the project midway, and Totto would have not been very happy. Coincidentally, Swinburne was hoping to join ME310 for the first time that year and had some funds for a first project. I asked Larry if he'd agree on working on a three-way collaboration on the Totto project together with Javeriana and Swinburne, and he agreed. Therefore, I managed to coach half of the Totto project from Javeriana, and the other half from Swinburne. From then on, Swinburne became an active member of the SUGAR Network, and its Design Factory Melbourne has collaborated in three projects with Stanford University.

Currently Lecturer at Swinburne University of Technology

Carlos Serrano, Ph.D.
ME310 global partner, AY2007–AY2010, AY2013

I started working in the course in 2007 when I retired from a private enterprise, Carvajal, from Cali. I moved to Javeriana University, Cali, to teach product design and to start as a student of fine arts. My background is chemical engineering, and I had worked all the time in R&D at Carvajal. So, the move sounded all too natural. I have enjoyed learning and practicing design thinking ever since then.

I came across the word SUGAR on one occasion, I believe in 2008, at Larry's office. He was telling Maria Camacho and myself about his idea of creating the international collaboration of universities with Stanford's ME310. He had some names on his board, including SUGA (without R). It occurred to me to tell Larry about the Cuban diva singer Celia Cruz, very famous in Latin America, who used to shout 'AZUCAR' in her interpretations. As you may know, azucar means sugar in Spanish. I even shouted SUGAR in front of Larry, to show him how Celia used to do it. Larry was very happy with the idea and the only thing he had to do was to accommodate the letter R to SUGA. This was how Larry decided to name the collaboration he had in mind as SUGAR. Afterwards, in every launch of a new ME310 course, if I was there, Larry would invite me to shout SUGAR — Celia Cruz style — in front of the audience.

Currently consulting

Christophe Vetterli, Ph.D.
ME310 global coach, AY2008–AY2012

> ❝ Two hours before the course application for the ME310 course in St. Gallen was due, I thought: 'ah, this opportunity sounds unusual: start-up environment, strategic challenge, diverse teams, inputs at Stanford. Let's try it!'

The early days of ME310 at the University of St. Gallen (HSG) started in 2005 by coincidence when Ernst Ensslin (former managing director of the Institute of Information Management) had contact with Philipp Skogstad who did an MBA in St. Gallen and told him about ME310. Ernst motivated Professor Walter Brenner to do a trip to Stanford and explore the possibilities. This was the initial start of ME310 at the University of St. Gallen. Bernhard Schindlholzer and Michael Klaas then started to operatively gather the first students and companies (the first three years with 1–3 teams).

I did my ME310 year at HSG in AY2008. I took over the coaching in 2009 — it was a critical time, because no one else was left to really do the job and coach the teams. I had the chance because Walter had confidence in me. I started to acquire new partners and introduce Falk Uebernickel onto the topic.

On that 'restarting' year, we acquired seven teams. I developed the operations of ME310 in St. Gallen from 2009 until 2013 — we initiated the SUGAR Network, started to create good knowledge in terms of process and business model design challenges to address with design thinking. I think it's not too exaggerated to say that those four years built the base for the current standing of St. Gallen in the SUGAR Network.

Ten years later as I write this, after having coached more than 50 design teams, every team with a minimum of 5 months each, and helping more than 40 companies to adopt this mindset, I am absolutely persuaded that this model started at Stanford is the future of addressing the challenges each company or industry has.

Currently Manager at Walkerproject AG

Falk Uebernickel, Ph.D.
ME310 global faculty, AY2008–AY2019, AY2012–AY2014

> ❝ Instead of bringing in more rigid structures, ME310 was embracing ambiguity and divergent thinking. I'm still excited about the almost magical effect of the method, which can turn even grey office rubbers into creative thinkers.

Anyone who has met me knows: I am enthusiastic about design thinking — whether at university, as a team member of my consulting firm ITMP, or in private. But that was not always the case! When I first heard about the method, I was very skeptical. Creativity, playful approaches and colorful post-its all didn't really fit with the structure and control I had acquired over the years as a trained financial accountant. Design Thinking has literally torn me out of this rigid thinking. The unique ability of the method to tackle wicked problems (i.e., solve complex questions) was an absolutely new and groundbreaking discovery for me. I realized the ultimate potential of the method, when we started developing new services and business models. Everything I knew, the rigid models and concepts, could not help. They were too structured, too narrow-minded and too far away from real customer needs.

Fascinated by Design Thinking, I also wanted to convince other people of the method's power. Alone? A matter of impossibility! Becoming part of ME310 was the logical step to achieve my goal. The network immediately convinced me with its striking arguments such as diversity, divergence from convergence, fast and iterative design of prototypes and provoking failures in order to learn. And, just like Larry Leifer always says: 'Defy gravity!'

For us as a business school in Switzerland, the ME310 model has created a unique yet familiar atmosphere. The University of St. Gallen was able to adapt ME310 to the requirements of services and business models and not only that. Today, we have expanded the tools to digital solutions as well.

What fascinates me about ME310 and its sister program SUGAR? I am still impressed that we have managed to grow from a program into a movement — exactly as Larry envisioned from the beginning — that is completely self-supporting and independently organized. This is only possible through the passion of the students, as well as the lecturers and our company participants around the globe, who work together on future innovations and — in one big team — shape the world of tomorrow.

The variety of company-sponsored challenges is unique. Over the last ten years, we have worked for almost all industries. Every challenge was different and demanded new ways to go to the limit of what is possible. For me, it is incredible to see so many successful ME310 and SUGAR products and services on the market that we have developed. And it's more than just our success that makes me exceedingly proud: all members are united by a true global friendship.

All the more reason we have to spread our success-leading principles, the unique way of thinking, and the positive attitude we share to gain new friends, further expand our network, and become even more diverse. We need to give more people a chance to learn ME310, SUGAR and — in general — human-centered design. So far, we have never worked with an African university. We need to fix this!

Currently Adjunct Professor for Information Management and Business Innovation at University of St. Gallen

Matteo Vignoli, Ph.D.
ME310 global faculty, AY2014

> Once you are in the river, you go with the flow. My flow was to bring back Design Thinking and ME310 to Italy and to the world. For this reason, this was my mission.

ME310 is about life, a deep river of energy that flows through the bright minds of talented people around the world. Once you drink from the source, you are part of it forever. This is how I have been feeling since 2010 when I had the privilege of being a visiting scholar at the Center of Design Research at Stanford University. Stanford is the innovators' kindergarten, and for me, it was like coming back to life: what it means to be a human, to be present, to empathize and to create. There I discovered Design Thinking, which is the language to speak about the future, the global language of innovation.

Design Thinking was new to my country, but Italy was ready for it. The University of Modena and Reggio Emilia (UNIMORE) was the first university to join the global SUGAR Network, and we have had projects since 2011. During the years, we worked with Audi (Switzerland – 2011), eFM (Finland – 2012), Forsa (Colombia – 2013), Iconsulting (Italy – 2013), Manutencoop MPSS (USA/Stanford – 2014), Nestlè (France – 2015), Sonae (Portugal – 2015), Yanmar (Japan – 2016), Bosch (France – 2016), DKV (Germany – 2017) and YNAP (Italy – 2017).

'Educate to Innovate' became our claim, and we merged Design Thinking with our Reggio approach, focusing on an issue that is important to us and to our society: our responsibility toward young people and toward future engineers.

In the new global economies, there is a growing need for people who can create new things. People who have not simply gained knowledge readily available on the Internet, but people that know how to use it in new ways. People able to deal with a wide sphere of possibilities, to understand problems, to find solutions, and to make decisions. People able to connect together other people, information, tools, companies and cultures, because that is how you create more value today.

I feel ME310 evolved into SUGAR, which is the unique global innovation platform. Over 40 universities around the world are connected by trust and experience. The power of the network is the exponential growth and our commitment for the next 50 years of ME310 is to grow SUGAR into the most powerful tool to shape the future of our society through the education of students and companies to the power of Design Thinking Innovation.

Currently Assistant Professor at University of Modena and Reggio Emilia

Leif Næss, Ph.D.
ME310 global faculty, AY2012

> The funniest prototype was the acceleration feedback prototype using a water-filled aquarium taped to the dashboard of one of the team members' car.

Our ME310 project targeted the key issues pertaining to the so-called 'range anxiety' of electric vehicle (EV) drivers. In 2012, 2.9 percent of the total number of new car purchases in Norway were zero-emission cars (i.e., battery electric vehicles or BEVs). The number of EV purchases per inhabitant was the highest in the world and 10 times higher than any other country. A project scope was established in the industry cluster Electric Mobility Norway (EMN) and funded by the Norwegian Centre of Expertise Systems Engineering (NCE-SE) in Kongsberg, Sweden.

The international project team of nine members was established between Stanford University, Norwegian University of Science and Technology (NTNU), and Buskerud University College (BUC) in September 2012. I was impressed by the team's broad skill base ranging from mechanical engineering, via industrial design and marketing, to electro-technical and hardware/software solutions. On EMN's side, Qfree, a company focusing on novel solution in traffic management, and Sintef Transportation, doing research in traffic management systems design and operation, were chosen as the most suitable industry partners for the project team.

The Norwegian EV market was a very early opportunity to explore range anxiety within a rapidly growing user basis. As such, the regional area between Oslo and Kongsberg, plus Trondheim, were new arenas for hypothesis testing and validation with a sufficient user basis. An early user study quickly revealed a surprising fact that range anxiety was not an issue among experienced EV drivers. This lead to the hypothesis that range anxiety pertained only to early EV users and would-be EV users. Hence, the typical pivoting and reformulation in the Stanford ME310 innovation process changed the project focus from 'mitigating range anxiety' to 'increase new EV drivers' confidence'.

Seen in hindsight, the pivot was a natural consequence of a user-centered approach and needed active facilitation to persuade Qfree and Sintef, as well as both EMN and NCE-SE clusters at large. This facilitation took place in the first face-to-face interactions at Kongsberg at Christmastime and well into the 'Dark Horse' phase of the student project. As such, I regard the pivot to be the most influential event in the project for the industry partners' under-standing of innovation processes. Also, the learning was key for how BUC developed the electives Product, Process, and Global Business innovation for their Masters in Business Administration (MBA) program.

The students initially thought they needed an emotional feedback component. The first idea they thought of was having one student's dear fish swimming in a bowl while someone was driving… in order to make a driver feel sad when the driving wasn't smooth enough. The second emotional component was a buzzer on the hairband.

Project execution was impressive. The team combined their broad skill base with extreme enthusiasm. The team members really knew the devils were in the details and used hypothesis formulations, practical testing, analysis with consequent conclusions, and actions to drive the product innovation. Their final product 'Crusie' provided feedback to the EV driver on their current driving style in action was based on a multitude of testing of several prototypes. All details of the products including a motivational gamification app and promotion material were designed and produced by team. Their stand at the EXPE was very well attended.

Buskerud University College, now the University of South-Eastern Norway, has used this experience in several project teams later through the SUGAR Network. The learning has also inspired us to endeavor into user-centered design at our Systems Engineering master's program. We now cooperate with the Norwegian School of Architecture and Design in Oslo in a cross-industry R&D program called Human Systems Engineering Framework. Here we explore possibilities to pivot between user-centered design, knowledge-based product development, and the systems engineering framework to improve and speedup product innovation in four very different industry companies in Norway.

And as for the EV penetration in Norway, 21.9% of all vehicles purchased in 2017 were BEVs with an on-the-road population of 5.1% zero-emission vehicles!

Currently Institute Leader, Norwegian Institute of Systems Engineering, at University of South-Eastern Norway

Tobias Larsson, Ph.D.
ME310 global faculty, AY2012–current

Having taken part in ME310 as a global academic partner for some 15 projects, it has been extremely rewarding. Over the years, we have used ME310 as a 'sandbox' for testing ways to collaborate between global companies, academic researchers, and young, hungry students with their careers ahead. We've explored, and learnt, how to 'see' and grade individual contribution in 'ill-defined' real projects, while still pushing a team to arrive at a final concept. We've explored different ways of supporting teams in distance collaboration, collaborative work, and also with engineering design tools. Some years have been better; some have had opportunity for improvement; but all have been rewarding and had a true impact on how we deploy capstone project courses at our university.

We've also seen that the ME310 curriculum challenges the 'normal', creating lively discussions among our faculty locally on roles in teaching and ways forward in the educational system. It is a repetitive, constantly improving process of innovating new solutions to the problems that are out there. Overall, the ME310 curricula and the Stanford way of engineering design / design thinking has had a great impact on how we look at learning and the way we set up course projects today.

Currently Chaired Professor in Mechanical Engineering at Blekinge Institute of Technology

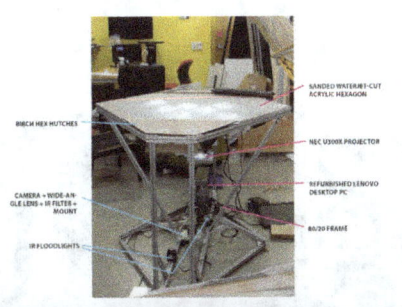

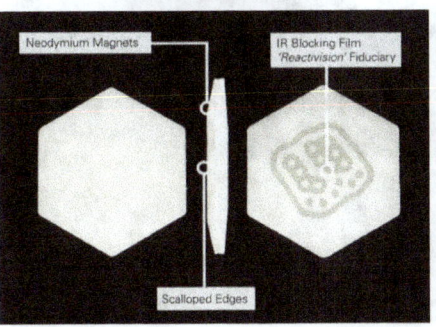

Yvonne Martin Rygiert
DSN 310 W student, spring 2017

The interactive online ME310 version [*called DSN 310 W and offered by Stanford's Continuing Studies Program — editor*] was unique for me because we were participating in the class individually and as part of a globally distributed team, sharing a common design challenge. This duality on an online format made the class very special.

I would start highlighting the team collaboration tools as being key during the 10 weeks that we worked together, and I have taken them with me after this class. We incorporated a language approach to build on others' ideas and noticed that group conversation on Skype requires different skills than when you share the same physical space. Also we learnt how to gather individual work and ideas to create a team assignment. On a personal note, I enjoyed the Buddy Checks exercise, and I often visualize the ladder when giving feedback to other projects.

Also it was enriching to see how my colleagues prototyped the ideas we had discussed as a team. As a distributed team, where there is no physical common space for everyone, we prototyped individually based on what we had shared during the Skype meetings. Afterwards, we shared the results and built the team's assignment. We each prototyped differently, and we brought different perspectives / approaches to the final team prototype.

The class has impacted my approach to ambiguity, to dance with it, and see how it is different from uncertainty, as well as gave me more knowledge on design tools like prototyping.

Currently consulting

The Students

1960s

The 1960s saw the early rise of computers, and Stanford University founded its Computer Science Department in 1965. The university dedicated the Stanford Linear Accelerator Center (SLAC) in 1967, and Kenneth Pitzer started as Stanford's sixth president in 1968. In the broader United States, the Vietnam War was ongoing, the Cuban Missile Crisis occurred in 1962, and U.S. President John F Kennedy was assassinated in 1963. It was also a decade of Civil Rights protests, and Martin Luther King Jr. was assassinated in 1968. The Beatles music phenomenon and a rise of a counter-cultural movement occurred mid-decade. Russia began the Space Race in 1961, leading to the U.S. putting the first man on the moon by 1969. — *Editor*

Gary Anderson
ME310 student, AY1967

> Professor Jim Adams was my faculty advisor, and I took many classes from him, along with Bob McKim, Bernie Roth, William Reynolds, and others inside the old Engineering corner. I also remember Larry Leifer as a teaching assistant.

We occasionally had a guest lecturer; I remember Jim Hall of Chaparral racing car fame come in to talk to us about horsepower, wings, and ground effect aerodynamics. I took all three sections of ME219 [*now listed as ME310 – editor*], and the eight units of A outweighed the D that I got in Advanced Thermo.

As you know, it was not all classroom, lab and field work in ME then. In one student/prof backyard patio Bar-B-Q, one of our TAs [*Teaching Assistants — editor*] decided that a trash can lid was aerodynamically equal to a Frisbee. I regret I got no images of those great professors and their comments on the lid launch.

After my M.S. in 1968, I went to work as a rocket scientist in the U.S. Navy Lab in China Lake, then as a mechanical engineer in Long Beach, CA. I earned my P.E. [*Professional Engineering – editor*] license and took off for Spain in 1981 to begin my international career with the U.S. Department of Defense (DoD) and Naval Facilities Engineering. I continued working for DoD for 40+ years, with stops along the way in San Diego and also Naples, Italy, and Sigonella, Sicily, with projects all over Western Europe and North Africa.

I retired as a senior mechanical engineer for the U.S. Navy in San Diego in 2009, and my wife Maria-Gracia and I returned to live in her hometown of Madrid, Spain. It is good to live in Europe, but we continue to get to California when we can. It has been several years since I've been on campus, but each time I visit, I'm pleased to see that progress continues. I'll miss the UGLY and the foundry, but will always have time to linger at Mem Claw or meander through the bookstore on White Plaza. No more bowling alleys or pool tables, but the cappuccino is still good at Tresidder.

Currently retired

1970s

At Stanford, the 1970s started with Richard Lyman taking office as its seventh president. Major political events in this decade were the energy OPEC crisis in the early 1970s, anti-war demonstrations and the end of the Vietnam War by 1975, the Watergate scandal and first U.S. presidential resignation, Iran hostage crisis, and a severe worldwide economic recession. Modern computing was born with the invention of the integrated circuit. Other big developments were email, lasers, pocket calculators, Sony Walkman, fiber optics, microwave ovens, cell phones, and the first supersonic flight. Apple was founded in 1976. This was also the golden age of video arcade games. Disco music peaked by decade end. — *Editor*

Warren Seering, Ph.D.
ME310 student, AY1972; ME310 coach, AY1973–AY1974

> ❝ Change had been ongoing since 1957, inspired by John Arnold's revolutionary ideas about engineering and design and enabled by the hiring of new design faculty in the early 1960s and the consequent development of new design classes.

The Stanford campus was charged with the energy of dissent at the beginning of the 1972–73 academic year. Disruptive protests of the Viet Nam war had occurred the previous spring. The Art Gallery and other buildings had been damaged by the protesters and were still boarded up. The Stanford Research Institute, now SRI International, had been separated from Stanford University because of ongoing research there in support of the war effort. Political differences triggered animated discussions among both students and faculty.

No one was quite sure whether the campus would settle into the term or erupt once again. Though the former proved to be the case, the heightened level of political engagement at Stanford, motivated by students with draft numbers, a situation that ended the following year, and interspersed with the attitudes and behaviors of the late 1960s San Francisco social revolution that had tripped down the peninsula and found Stanford to be a welcoming hostess, yielded a campus culture in which change was seen to be as inevitable as its direction was uncertain. This Stanford culture was also embedded in the Design Division at that time.

When John Arnold came to Stanford from MIT in 1957, he introduced the class, Mechanical Engineering Design, and then a series of graduate design classes that emphasized human-centered design and design creativity. He also established the Design Division in the Department of Mechanical Engineering. Jim Adams was one of Arnold's Ph.D. students. Jim graduated in 1961, worked at JPL, and returned to the Design Division in 1966, becoming its director in 1968. Throughout the 1960s, the Design Division grew — faculty were hired, and courses were added in ways that expanded the vision of engineering design that Arnold had framed.

The faculty were enthusiastically committed to transforming the products of this growth into an innovative way of thinking about engineering design and design education, one organized around the potential user of the designed product and employing creativity to enrich the space of design options. They had decided to use the existing three-quarter graduate course sequence, ME219, as a platform for their experiment in design education.

In the Fall term of 1972, the course sequence was merged with several other graduate design classes to become an integrated, year-long experimental course sequence called ME201: Advanced Engineering Design.

The enthusiasm for the sequence was evident on the first day with seven design faculty members participating in the introductory lecture. Thirty-two students made up the nine project teams. Jim Adams coordinated the effort the first year with the assistance of John Manning, Bernie Roth, and the rest of the Design faculty including Bob McKim, Henry Fuchs, Bill Verplank, and Bob Piziali. Doug Wilde moved from Chemical Engineering to join the Design Division the following spring. Following this trial run, the sequence was given the number ME210 and then in time ME310.

In the 1960s and early 1970s, design engineering was generally not perceived to be a creative, collaborative, or user-oriented discipline. Design courses focused on the physics of machine components. Numerous aspects of the new ME201 course sequence were seen as revolutionary at the time but have subsequently become conventional practice. Much was made early in the course of the need for design engineers to collaborate with manufacturing engineers in defining the form of the product. There was a strong emphasis early in the sequence on breaking down the metaphorical wall between design and manufacturing. Convention at the time had engineers responsible for designing to meet the product specifications that they were given. In ME201, students were encouraged to challenge the product ideas that the project sponsors brought and to think in creative ways to identify superior solutions. The course was organized around a set of engineering projects submitted mostly by corporate sponsors which were to serve as active learning case studies of the design process.

In retrospect, though, the biggest new idea introduced in the class was that engineers should focus on understanding the needs of the user of the product before they designed it. There were no chapters on need-finding in design textbooks prior to the Stanford experiment. And it wasn't until the early 1980s, when Toyota engineers were 'caught' observing users in parking lots loading groceries into their trunks, that U.S. manufacturers, who at first challenged the practice as giving Toyota an unfair advantage, began to take seriously the process of having engineers gather user needs, the process that had been taught and practiced in the Advanced Engineering Design sequence, by then titled ME210, for more than a decade.

Another valuable aspect of the class grew from the fact that for the projects there were no right answers. As a consequence, students got to see the faculty as role models, using the methods that they were teaching as they collaborated with the students to develop designs and solve the design problems that arose while trying to satisfy the customers.

Currently Professor of Mechanical Engineering at MIT

ME 215A, B, C	Design Seminar	not available – in 201
ME 218	Control System Components & Synthesis	not available – in 206 sequence
ME 219A	Advanced Engineering Design	not available – in 201
ME 219B	Design Operations	not available – in 201
ME 219C	Experimental Development Engineering	not available – in 201
ME 220	Computer Aided Design	available next year – also in 201
ME 221	The Individual and Technology	not available – in 201
ME 222	Kinematic Synthesis of Mechanisms	available next year on
ME 223	Advanced Kinematics	available next year on
ME 225	Fluid Power Control	available this & alternate years
ME 227	Topics in Unsteady Gasdynamics	not available
ME 228	Fluidics	available next & alternate years
ME 235A, B	Engineering Systems Design	available next year on

Tim Hight, Ph.D.
ME310 student, AY1972

The graduate design course sequence that I took in 1972–73 school year (I think it was ME210 in those days) was a revelation and, to a large extent, was the foundation for the design courses that I have taught throughout my career. Bernie Roth, Doug Wilde, Jim Adams — what an introduction to design! In my first academic position at Duke University, I blended some of the notions of design process into a one-semester machine design course, but it was here at Santa Clara University that I was able to fully implement a yearlong senior design course with many of the elements from ME210. Since the late '80s, we have put our senior MEs [*Mechanical Engineering students — editor*] through a comprehensive design-build-test project experience with teams tackling problems from industry, faculty, or sponsored contests.

Probably a third of the lectures and exercises that we do can be traced back to that Stanford graduate design course. I even have them read *Zen and the Art of Motorcycle Maintenance*, which I still find to be a compelling and thought-provoking book for seniors about to make a living as engineers.

Currently Chair of the Mechanical Engineering Department and Associate Professor at Santa Clara University

David Kelley
ME310 student, AY1975

My project was with Xerox PARC, and we were building a mechanism in order to automatically read microfiche. Bob Piziali was the advisor... I do remember it being successful, but I do not remember much more!

Currently Professor of Mechanical Engineering at Stanford University and founder of IDEO

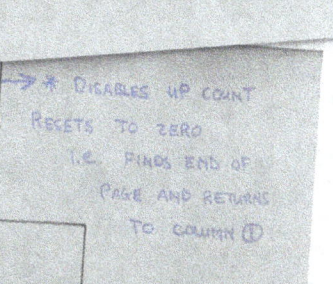

FINAL PROBLEM STATEMENT

To design a microfiche indexing system and totally adapted reader that:

1. performs the most common operations needed when reading a microfiche, which are: step forward and backward; index up and down; proceed to successive page at the end of a row; and referral to a previous page.
2. has a simple and straightforward user interface.
3. operates on one size microfiche, 105mm x 148mm, approximately 4 x 6 inches, one reduction ratio of 48X, COM (computer output microfilm).
4. when incorporated into a complete reader, will market for $500 to $700. This would attract a market between the two extremes of existing microfiche systems.
5. is capable of being adapted to an existing reader with good quality optics, and find a correspondingly appropriate platen.
6. access each successive page within .25 seconds, to make reading microfiche an efficient process.
7. fine tuning ability, to initially adjust the framing of an image, or to center a desired portion of a page.

Tom Cooper
ME310 student, AY1976

The class was a chance to work on a project that was semi-realistic, where we had to understand needs, and then design and build a device to meet those needs. It was good experience working with others and working in the shop. We had to demonstrate the device at the end. Our project was a wheelchair that could raise and lower, tilt, and get narrower. It was rather dangerous to use if I recall correctly. I wish I had pictures but don't. I designed the tilt mechanism. Robert Piziali was the teacher. I think our group had 5 people.

Currently a Fellow at Intuitive Surgical

Jeff Lotz
ME310 student, AY1979

We focused mostly on the hands-free aspect of the technology and developed some prototypes for a neck-worn device. I remember our schematic showing neck-worn phones linked wirelessly to communication hubs placed on phone poles. Also remember our sponsor David Thornburg's process of innovating by playing with various bits of random materials he kept in his office — plus his goofy leather brimmed hat. Other team projects were impressive, like the self-guided wheel chair that tracked walls using ultrasound.

Currently Professor of Orthopaedic Surgery and Vice Chair of Research at University of California San Francisco

Laird Cagan
ME310 student, AY1979

I remember the class and the project with Jeff Lotz and Diane Riker. The evolution of the portable phone (cell phone) turned out to be one of the most important/valuable inventions on the planet. I wish I had carried it further!

Currently Managing Director and Co-Founder, Cagan McAfee Capital Partners

ABSTRACT

PROBLEM STATEMENT

To design, test, and build a wireless telephone. The only design criteria were that it should:

1. be so portable that it would be as comfortable to have around as clothing
2. interface with existing telephones.

The design team was to choose the applications and determine the important human factors.

THE DESIGN APPROACH

The application of the design was limited to a business environment. It was further decided that the telephone should be operated without the use of the hands (exclusive of dialing) and that no part of the telephone should extend above the jaw.

The team analyzed many types of sound transmission including speaker arrays, bone conduction, earphones, and cylindrical tube propagation, then examined potential configurations for each.

RESULTS

The most feasible system is shown below. It is worn around the neck with the sound projected through a cylindrical tube toward the user's ear. The privacy of the system is excellent, as is the convenience and reliability; unfortunately, the design requires approximately four times the power of presently existing systems. The microphone is located at the top of the base unit which houses the electronic components and power supply. The antenna is in the neck strap.

WALLET PHONE

DESCRIPTION

This is a completely portable unit designed to fit jacket pockets, as shown in figures 10 and 11. The front panel opens to reveal the dial pad and speaker. Sound is channeled by the front panel (in the open position) to a small receiver. The antenna retracts into the bottom of the unit when not in use.

REASONS FOR REJECTION

1. Requires two hand operation.

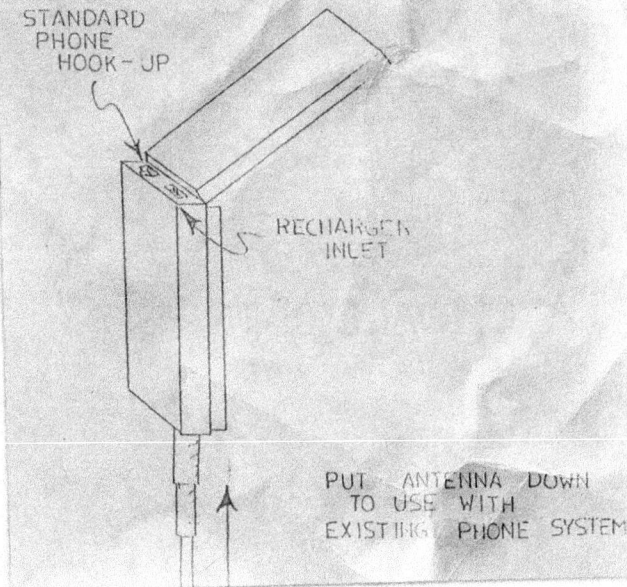

1980s

The 1980s started with Donald Kennedy as Stanford's eighth president. The decade included the Cold War ending between the U.S. and Russia, the Chernobyl nuclear disaster and Challenger space explosion in 1986, the Iran–Iraq War, and the fall of the Berlin Wall in 1989. The personal computing industry exploded this decade with the inventions of a graphical user interface and computer mouse. By the late 1980s, Nintendo had revived the video game industry, and gene therapy techniques were first done. Japanese and Korean companies entered the U.S. auto market, and fuel injection replaced carburetors. MTV launched, and music videos became popular. In 1989, the Loma Prieta earthquake caused extensive damage at Stanford. — *Editor*

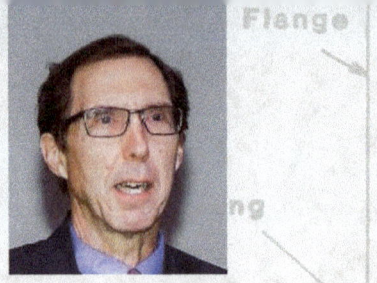

Eric Byler, Ph.D.
ME310 student, AY1983; sponsor, AY1987–AY2010; director, AY2017–current

> The ME310 team discovered that Integration & Test drove 50% of the cost (and schedule)... their approach saved about $25 million of labor per satellite, or about $150 million per year.

I took ME210 in AY1983 with Prof. Phil Barkan, five years out of undergrad. The loft was on the 5th floor of Terman, way in the back by the stairs. (Terman had no A/C so the loft got pretty hot.) Our project was to build an end-effector for a Cincinnati Milacron T3 robot (a state-of-the-art system) for an operating manufacturing line to drill large holes through very thick aluminum structures at random, funny angles, while avoiding drill-tip spin-off, binding, and other issues. The hardest part was making a hemispherical bearing in Dave Beach's shop; the most fun part was visiting the factory in San Jose. Toward the end of spring quarter, when the stress level was rising, we were offered one-hour trips in the Imaginarium — a 5m dome with 2pi str. ~seamless video, music, and aroma sprays that was previously used (before being outlawed) to study the benefits of LSD on engineering designers. The experience provided some of us with amazing clarity and refreshment; others fell asleep from exhaustion.

Three years later, in 1987, I sponsored my first project with ME210 as a corporate liaison for a robotic end-effector to help assemble the International Space Station. The project was a success, but our company lost the proposal, so the hardware never flew in space. In the 1990s and 2000s, I funded three more ME310 space projects involving different types of satellites and mechanisms. Each successive project provided more and more benefits as I grew from an engineer to a manager to a director, and understood the broader business benefits available from sponsoring an ME310 project. It was always refreshing to leave my window-less building and come to Stanford to be inspired by the students!

My last sponsored project (in 2011) was the most successful: the re-architecting of a communications satellite. When I proposed the idea to the executive team in my company's C-suite, they said it was pointless — obviously you need 30+ years of experience in satellite design, and the Stanford students didn't even know space (radiation, thermal, etc.)! However, the ME310 team discovered that Integration & Test drove 50% of the cost (and schedule), so they developed a new approach to assembly. Their new prototype unfolded and folded like a Lotus flower, especially useful for backtracking failed tests when costs are extremely high. This approach saved about $25 million of labor per satellite, or about $150 million per year.

But the critical part of the

project was yet to come — our company's chief architect would not accept the design. Luckily, there had been extensive discussions throughout the year with company engineering directors, factory technicians, and test engineers. When the executive team started asking for internal validation, they received overwhelming support. My takeaway is that strategic management of your liaison activities and team is critical.

Now, retired from business, as ME310 executive director for project development, I help guide companies through the sponsorship process and show them the wide range of benefits available. Having spent my last 10 years managing large development portfolios, Larry Leifer thought I could provide a 'broadband connection' between academia and business needs. I love the wide range of projects that come in every year, and the projects are as fun as ever!

Currently ME310 Executive Director at Stanford University

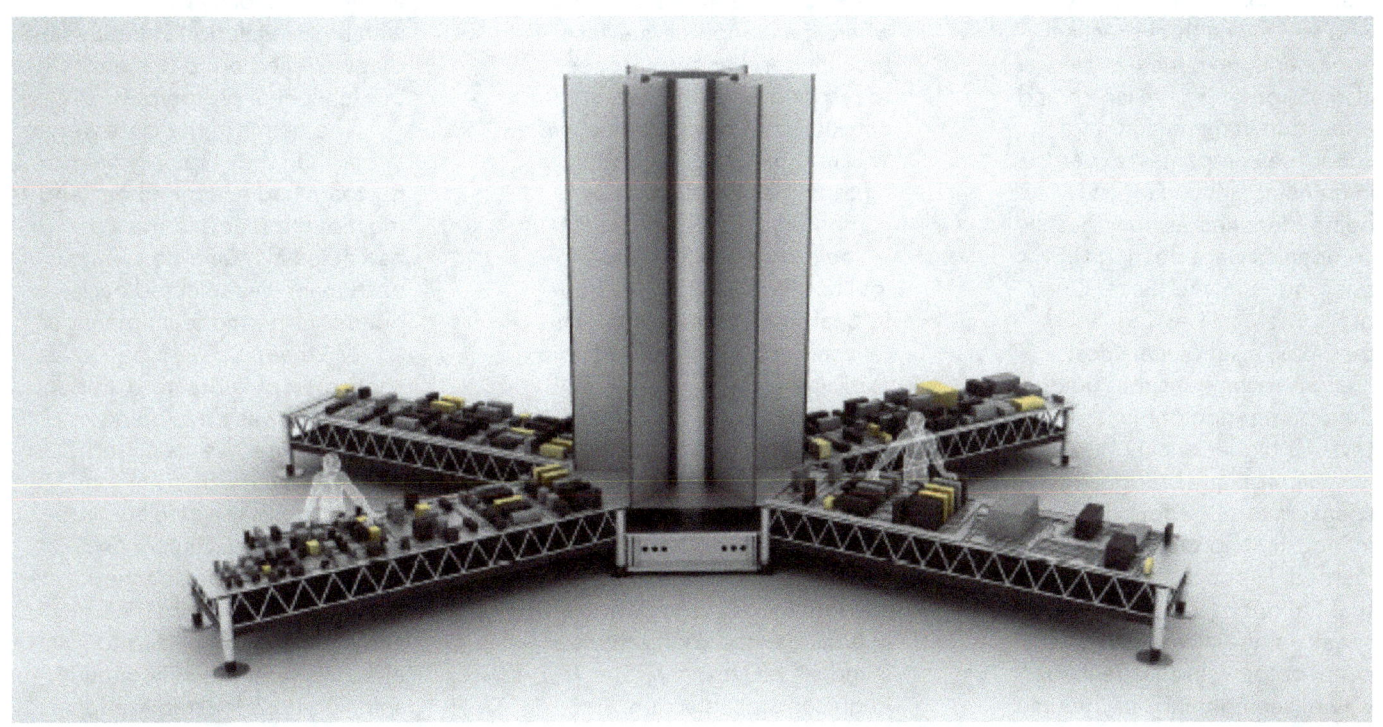

David Cannon, Ph.D.
ME310 student, AY1986; ME310 coach, AY1990, AY1992–AY1995

> While we had our share of disagreements, teams generally remained on good terms even after the class was over. I still occasionally see and say hi to a few of the people I met through the class, several decades later.

When I took the class in AY1986, it was designated ME210, and Phil Barkan taught it. Phil was a good-natured, realistic, unassuming professor who had a wealth of practical engineering experience. He was also a promoter of research and education in manufacturing; Japanese companies' expertise in manufacturing was just being identified as how these companies were beating U.S. ones in the marketplace. One of his interests was Taguchi methods, a set of statistical analysis techniques that guide the optimization of manufacturing towards higher quality.

He regularly brought in speakers to talk about their work in industry and the lessons they'd learned. I know I didn't get all that I might have out of these speakers; their lessons didn't connect to my inexperienced way of seeing things at the time. But as I've recalled some of them in later years, they've been more meaningful. I recall an IBM engineer who talked about how they discovered a ~2-second rule, where if a computer interface took longer than about 2 seconds to respond, then the user's productivity would fall off a cliff. This resulted in IBM allocating more of their production of computers for internal use. Many of the other speakers told of 'political' issues that they had to deal with in their work. This reflected a truth that's been more explicitly emphasized in ME310 as time has gone on — that interpersonal dealings affect technical work everywhere.

Many of the things taught in the class, and that were the subject of course assignments, were methods commonly used in engineering organizations in industry: Gantt charts, Pugh concept selection, morphological analysis, and such. We regularly made illustrative prototypes. There was also a CAD system we could use, with limited-availability CAD terminals with high-resolution color displays that we relied on to design our functional prototypes.

The teams in the class were larger than they typically are now: my team had five members, and most of the teams in the class had at least 4. One person on each team was selected each quarter to be the team manager.

My team project was sponsored by a Stanford student group that was developing a small satellite. We designed and tested a mechanism that could fit, with the satellite, into a 'Get-Away-Special', or GAS can, that would be attached just inside a space shuttle's bay and launched. It needed to just eject the satellite on command, spinning it up for stabilization.

Because it was a student-led project, we got a few breaks around campus. We were allowed to use some space in a lab to build and test our functional prototype, and one of the teachers in the student shop (now PRL) agreed to give us a discount on machining the critical pieces of our prototype — he was just interested in seeing it work. We ended up writing and presenting a conference paper on the design and test results after the class was over.

For several years between 1998 and 2003 in Spring quarter, I taught a design class to engineering and science students participating in study abroad at the Stanford Japan Center (SJC) in Kyoto, Japan. There was, in the Kyoto/Kansai area, a kind of club consisting of Japanese professionals who had studied at or been visiting researchers at Stanford. Every year they'd throw a nice lunch for the students and staff who were at the SJC.

One prominent club member was a high-level executive at Toray Industries, a Japanese chemistry-oriented multinational company that started out in the 1920s making rayon. Today they employ 45,000 people. Being a high-level executive in the company is a big deal. He would often invite a few people over to have dinner at his place during that quarter, to talk about what was going on at Stanford and to reminisce. I was invited one year, and as we talked, he found out that I had been involved in the ME310 class, and that he had taken the class while he was there — in the late 1960s or early 1970s; I forget the exact year.

He then went into another room and brought back some clippings from the *Stanford Daily* newspaper, that included one or two pictures of him and others in the class with a boat at Lake Lagunita. They'd built the boat out of some ridiculously inadequate set of materials, and the team had raced it on the lake — rather similar to the way that the paper bike race is done. His team had done well, if I recall, and the camaraderie he experienced helped him feel like he could make it through the course, and through the degree, at Stanford.

Two other things I picked up from his story. One, the early crash course in team building that is the paper bike race had a kind of precedent. And two, for this Japanese executive, the race on the lake was one of the highlights of his time at Stanford — he talked very warmly and happily about it and had kept those newspaper clippings for something like 30 years.

I also learned about the challenges of being a team coach. For example, one class project was in aerospace design, in which I have a little experience, and I had met one of the students before she started a master's degree. It made sense for me to become their coach.

There soon came stretches where the two students could hardly hold an important conversation about the project, in which some decision needed to be made without it turning into a heated argument. I ended up stepping in as a kind of half team-member. I tried several things to get them to ease up — for instance, if they had a complaint, then it first had to be a complaint to me, and about me. I also sometimes took the role, not common for a coach, of insisting on things being done as agreed, rather than just being an advisor. That way, they could blame me for being too harsh, rather than digging into each other. The quality of their interaction swung back and forth.

The two continued to work together until the middle of the third quarter, then just couldn't keep going. In the end, one of them actually finished the project, and then went on to do his Ph.D. work by further building, testing, and operating the artificial star for calibrating the satellite, working closely with the project liaison. The other has gone on to teach design at places like Yale.

Currently Postdoctoral Researcher at NASA Langley Research Center

Ade Mabogunje, Ph.D.
ME310 student, AY1988; coach, AY1990, AY1992–AY1993; T.A., AY1991

> My long involvement with ME310 is a long story, but the short version was best expressed by the late Phil Barkan, who taught the class from 1980 to 1986. Phil called ME310 a microcosm of Silicon Valley.

I enrolled in ME310 in the fall of 1988 (then it was called ME210). After two weeks, I dropped the class, opting for ME231A — Dynamics, a class taught by Thomas Kane. A week later, I met with Larry Leifer to ask if I can enroll again. He agreed.

Why did I drop ME310 for ME231? ME231 was more in line with what I felt was the model for engineering classes. Why did I return? My friend Folabi Esan, who was in the Manufacturing Systems Engineering program, and also taking ME310, thought my decision to leave did not make sense, especially since all of our engineering classes in Nigeria were like ME231. Why not take ME310 where you are given the opportunity, means, and freedom to work on a challenging industry problem that is of value to real people? This made a lot of sense, so I re-enrolled. From that time on, I have been a student, a coach, a teaching assistant, a researcher, and an exporter of ME310, to other departments in Stanford, and later to Nigeria and India.

I did my bachelors studies in Nigeria and graduated with a first class in Mechanical Engineering. During my studies, I had the opportunity to work with Siemens in Germany as part of my industrial training program (ausbildung). After graduation, I worked for several years in the oil industry in Nigeria before coming to Stanford for graduate studies. My purpose was to understand how computers could be used to accelerate development in developing countries.

At the end of my first quarter at Stanford, I felt I had some insight into what made engineering at Stanford different from my experience in Nigeria, Germany, and France. For example, Americans ask questions differently. I came up with the assertion that design is a question-driven process. Thus, if computers were to be used to accelerate development, they needed to augment and support the question-asking process. This process is rooted in human curiosity, and this constitutes the thread through my work. Now, most regions of the world have a proverb that is similar to the English saying 'curiosity kills the cat'. Well, that is what ME310 is: how to harness human curiosity to create value for others and be a cat with many lives.

During the first week of the class, we participated in a design communication workshop run by Scott Minneman. Scott was a graduate student of Larry, who was also working part time at Xerox PARC. The workshop was recorded on video, and the video records formed part of the data for Scott's Ph.D. thesis. This was cool! I had never observed myself solving problems in a group before. I was curious to find out more about his work.

For my industry project, my teammate was Victor Sanchez, and our industry liaison was Hisup Park from Lockheed Missiles & Space Company in Sunnyvale, and our coach was John Kimball, a career designer in the aircraft industry. Our challenge was to design a system that prevented the aluminum sheets used in missile design from kinking during manufacture.

I was a teaching assistant along with Margot Brereton in 1991–92. Larry had taken a sabbatical year off to do a start-up company. The instructors that year were Bernie Roth and David Radcliffe, who was visiting from Queens University in Brisbane, Australia. The first quarter was quite an experience. We did a version of the paper bike race. This time, the race was going to be in the Terman pond, and so the mobility paper vehicles had to survive multiple trips around the pond immersed in water!

Over time through Larry, we shared models of the class with Terry Winograd in computer science, Renate Fruchter in Civil and Environmental Engineering, Paul Yock in the Biodesign program, and Cliff Nass in the Communications department, as well as Rolf Lenschow from NTNU in Norway, and Poul Hansen from Aalborg University in Denmark.

In 1997, Larry was awarded the ASME Teaching Innovation Award, and later in the year when Sheri Sheppard, Larry Friedlander, and Larry Leifer became co-directors of the Stanford Learning Lab, the model of ME310 spread further afield. Mark Cutkosky taught the class during this period, and after the transition of leadership at the learning lab, Larry L. and Mark began to co-teach the class.

In 2002, I began working with Cliff Nass and Syed Shariq in Stanford's School of Humanities and Sciences on a project named real-time venture design (ReveL). The project aimed to bring shared global prosperity through the design of sustainable entrepreneurial ventures; in short, we were exploring the chemistry of start-up companies. What makes some companies — such as HP, Medtronics, Apple — stand the test of time, while other companies fail in a very short time? Needless to say, every ME310 team is a potential start-up company. In order to drive home this point, it may be useful to return to the origin of the French word of 'entrepreneur'. The term entrepreneur, unlike the term business man, returns to the idea of realization of a project in the form of an organization. The term 'entrepreneur' uses the concepts of creation and of innovation, and therefore differs from that of the head of a company.'

In other words, in ME310 teams, we see the nucleus of innovation ecosystems like Silicon Valley. If one can imagine an additional academic quarter in which students are taught how to realize their projects as organizations, as well as are supported in this phase with various forms of capital, then innovation ecosystems can be nucleated and nurtured in other parts of the world.

In 2010, I started working with Neeraj Sonalkar, David Cannon, Malte Jung, and other partners in Silicon Valley to further these ideas in Nigeria and India. Neeraj developed a notational system that allows us to visualize the interaction dynamics of teams, David derived a correlation between the time-based dynamics of language use and team performance, and Malte did some very seminal work on the emotion of design teams. He is now at Cornell University.

My research in the last five years has focused on ways to accelerate the nucleation process, as this has been shown to have a direct effect on the capital formation process of a region. Part of this work has been supported by the Hasso Plattner Design Research Program and the Kauffman Foundation. As I conclude this ME310 retrospective, I must say it has been a wild, unexpected, and fulfilling ride. I remember Larry announcing in class in 1988: that in ME310, you will learn to do the work of 10 years in 1 year. At the time, I thought he was talking about learning efficiency.

Now I can see he was talking about extreme collaboration. There were 10 teams in the class, and his vision was one of maximum question asking, sharing, empathizing, prototyping, debating, and learning. Under these conditions, every team failed at some point. However, we did not all fail at the same time. So, we learned to build a community that supported each other. I am glad I re-enrolled in this class.

Currently a Senior Research Associate at Stanford University

Vinod Baya, Ph.D.
ME310 student, AY1989; ME310 coach, AY1993–AY1994, AY2012–current

> ME310 today continues to reinvent what design thinking is and how it infuses creativity into the engineering design process, even as the process changes with connectivity, distributed teams, and globalization.

How good is the education if it does not prepare you for the real world? How good is the education if it does not make you creative so you can solve real problems?

As I reflect on my association with ME310, off and on for over 27 years, these two questions above frame for me what ME310 is all about. It is about giving the students an education that prepares them for the real world and makes them creative, so that they can take on any challenge that comes their way.

I took the class in AY1989 when it was called ME210 and did a project for Ford Motor Corporation, designing a semi-active suspension with two of my fellow classmates. I had already completed a Bachelors and Master's degree in Mechanical Engineering and was working towards a Ph.D. However, ME210 was the first time that I faced a real-world problem, not just in the technical complexity it represented, but the organizational context of a client organization, a budget, making timely decisions, and delivering a fully functional solution, on time and under budget!

Working with the industry liaison and ME310 coach, we framed a problem that was of value to Ford. Unshackled by the institutional hierarchy, work culture, and barriers to innovation that commonly exist in most large corporations, we were free to dream and stretch ourselves, be creative, all for the benefit of Ford Motor Corporation. We were using design thinking approaches before they were called that, now in common use to drive innovation across the business world.

Ford was so happy with our solution and approach that they flew the full team to their facility in Detroit, and we presented the solution to a large group of engineers and executives. Ford even hired one of the team members. Everything that happened, I later learned, is how things happen in the real world. I can think of no other class in my education, which gave me such a realistic dose of what mechanical engineers do on a day to day basis. Although, my career path took me away from core engineering to technology analysis, consulting and innovation, what I learned in ME310 is something I routinely fall back on to understand innovation, product development, design and engineering.

Much is feared today, and has been for some time, about the education today. Businesses complain that the new hires do not have skills needed on the job and fresh graduates have to be trained before they are productive and useful to the business. At the same time, many leading thinkers suggest that education of today often educates students out of their creative ability by focusing on highly analytical and mechanistic learnings. In such a context, ME310 is a breadth of fresh air, and I look upon my experience as student and my association as industry coach with great fondness. ME310 truly provides a way out of these fears and develops engineers who gain real industry experience and develop their creative muscles.

Currently Head of Emerging Technologies at Citi

1990s

In 1992, Gerhard Casper became Stanford's ninth president. The 1990s also ushered in the independence of the former Soviet republics, while the Gulf War was fought from 1990–1991, and the Rwandan genocide occurred in 1994. Princess Diana died tragically in 1997. In technology, the Hubble space telescope was launched in 1990, and Dolly the sheep became the first mammal to be cloned from an adult somatic cell. In 1991, CERN publicized its World Wide Web project, and email and instant messaging became popular tools this decade. The first MP3 music player launched in 1997. Microsoft Windows operating systems dominated the software industry, and a fear of a "Y2K" computer malfunction created some hysteria through 1999. — *Editor*

Darren Bonnstetter
ME310 student, AY1990

> ME310 was free-flowing and very creative. I had never been in a class that allowed the students to think creatively and solve real problems. We all felt very motivated and wanted to help our sponsor succeed.

I recall how much I loved the new Macintosh computers and my first experience with Excel in the fall of 1990. Up until that point, I had only used Lotus 123 (and before that, VisiCalc).

Larry Leifer wore multi-colored reading glasses; he was not afraid to stand out with a fashion statement. I was impressed by Larry's passion, and he smiled every day. He drove home the point of 'rapid prototyping'. At that time, I worked at General Motors. I interpreted rapid prototyping as ordering parts that might arrive in 6 weeks. In Larry's world, that meant cutting linkages out of foam core or other cheap material and testing designs in hours.

We had to make bicycles out of paper and then race them. Our team created a very elaborate roller-bearing design that failed during the contest. I learned that getting a product to work on the intended launch date is better than a promise of something great that doesn't deliver.

I started sketching ideas in Larry's class and still use a sketchbook for crazy ideas. I also recall seeing the stereolithography machine in Terman, years ahead of public awareness of 3D printing. I would love to see what the teams are working on now, so I can see decades into the future. Larry introduced us to a company that did the special effects for the movie 'The Abyss'. I thought that was really cool.

After graduation, I returned to General Motors for a few years. I pushed for rapid prototyping of many new ideas, but I felt stifled by corporate inertia and bureaucracy. However, I still used the concept of 'moving fast' and was able to be very successful at GM: they sponsored me for an MBA at Harvard Business School.

I still see companies (such as the apparel industry) that fall into old habits of accepting very slow prototyping and product development. I consulted for a high-fashion clothing company that had a product development cycle of more than a year. The executives had accepted that amount of time as the status quo and could not comprehend the fast-fashion moves of Zara. I knew the secret, thanks to the teachings of Larry.

As a turnaround consultant today, I often found myself in companies that had thousands of problems. I would identify the biggest ones and use rapid prototyping concepts to test and implement change. For example, a steel company struggled with factory throughput. I identified a few bottlenecks (thanks to help from ME210 and ME217) and had some friendly mechanics help me alleviate the problems with some simple gear changes on a conveyor belt. The throughput increased immediately, and the employees were hailed as heroes. Getting a few quick wins motivated the team and allowed us to continue to tackle other difficult problems.

Then as the CEO of a $175M pet supply company, I used rapid prototyping in creative ways. I tested price increases on a few products, measured results, and then raised prices on thousands of products. This company had not raised prices in 5 years, but with rapid testing and implementation, we were able to drop millions to the bottom line. I also tested eliminating a few SKUs. I started with over 60,000 products and used the concepts of rapid prototyping to test and implement massive reductions, cutting to under 25,000. That allowed us to cut the number of warehouses in half, decrease stock-outs, and lowered our inventory by millions of dollars. Simultaneously, our sales growth increased because our customers had simplified choices. In addition, we launched a private label line of products. Our team sketched designs for aquariums, and we quickly built models. Within 6 months, we started selling a successful line of products that grew to a large percentage of our revenue.

I now work as President at Bowers & Wilkins, a high-end audio company. This company has a slow product development cycle, so perhaps I need to hire a few students from the ME310 class to help infuse some change!

Currently President at Bowers & Wilkins

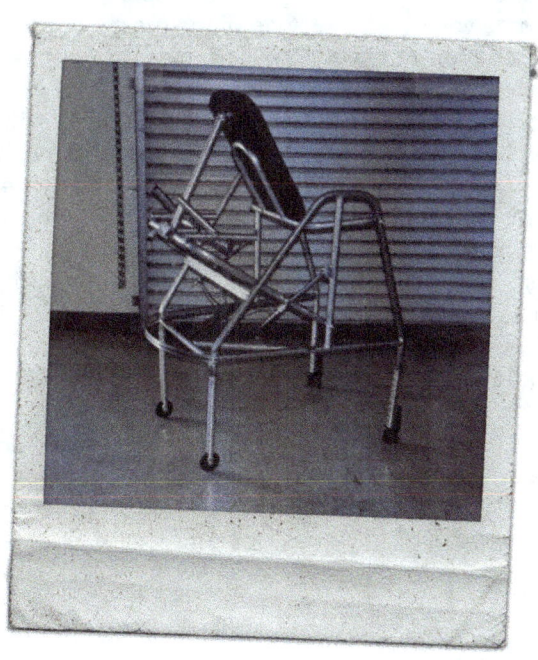

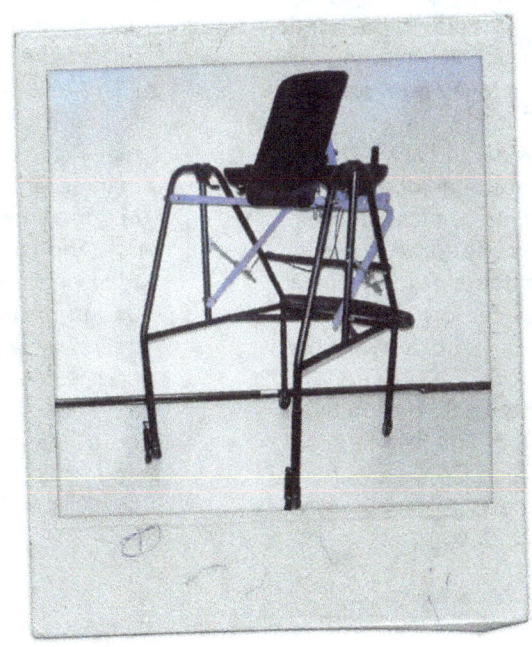

Rafay Khan
ME310 student, AY1991

> " The class with ambidextrous thinking allowed me to build products and later a business with an understanding that allowing for early iterative failures is critical for future success.

I took ME210 in 1991–92 despite being told by everyone that it be the toughest course and I would have no LIFE. Yes, we did win the Silver Medal [*from the James F. Lincoln Arc Welding Foundation awards program — editor*] on our team's four-wheel steering design. Fun project, and we drove the car to Larry Leifer's home, but the neighbors called in the police because of the racket it made as we drove it up to his home. And I believe his wife never forgave me.

Early in my career at Chrysler, I reduced design vibrations in steering wheel design by modeling 3-dimensional spring system using CAE software and iterated against a bench test. Got an engineering award for the work!

Later in my career as general manager at DigitalGlobe, I was asked to grow a business that had flat revenues for three years but was key to success on their IPO. I leveraged the 'diverge to converge' methodology that allowed us to identify core markets and doubled revenues in three years to $100M.

And I followed the design thinking process to first understand and observe customer needs by talking with the team and customers. Then I developed a number of 'Dark Horse' go-to-market strategies with a key understanding that we will need to measure success in real-time and will force ourselves — I call this the 'Groan Zone' — to drop a few strategies, not on how much we like them but on acceptance by customers. For example, one of the most interesting financial markets / hedge funds paled in comparison to success with urban planning demand from cities in Asia.

On implementing the above process, it isn't easy to get the team to accept the early time spent in divergent thinking and accepting complexity or the unknown, and then later picking the right strategies and doubling down on the winning strategies.

Currently CEO at Moove.ai

THE STANFORD DAILY
An Independent Newspaper

Designing an award-winning future

Rafay Khan was one of 18 graduate students who recently won awards in a program recognizing achievement in engineering design. He and Dan Wallace won a silver award for a steering system they designed for Ford Motor Co.

Engineering students win contest honors

By Sara Skinner

A hands-on class turned into money and recognition for 18 graduate students who won nine of 12 awards — including all the Gold, Silver and Bronze prizes — in a program recognizing achievement in engineering design.

Teams of students from a Stanford mechanical engineering design class dominated the winners list for the 1990-91 Professional Awards Program sponsored by the James F. Lincoln Arc Welding Foundation.

The foundation has offered the contest for the past 55 years. Stanford has won "at least half the awards" since first entering in 1979, according to teaching assistant Mike Strange. This year is "probably the best Stanford has ever done," he said.

The projects were a part of Prof. Larry Leifer's mechanical engineering 210 class in Graduate Design.

Students Greg Twiss and Gregg Patterson won the $1,000 Gold award for a rivet button measurement system designed for Boeing Corp. Twiss, who is preparing to earn his Ph.D in mechanical design, said the device will be used by inspectors to find weak spots in airplane joints.

Previously, he said, the measurement system only told whether the joint was good or bad. Twiss and Patterson created a portable pack that stores information on both the height and diameter of the rivets. This information can later be down-loaded into a computer and used to plot data on the joints.

Silver Awards went to Darren Bonnstetter and Carol Smallwood for a walking rehabilitation device for the Veteran's Administration, and to Rafay Khan and Dan Wallace for a steering system for Ford Motor Co.

Smallwood, who now works for Hewlett-Packard, said the walking device uses a design similar to a climber's harness to catch patients if they fall, and the angle of the device can be changed to help patients stand straighter as rehabilitation progresses.

The device is designed for adults who are learning to walk again after hip surgery, a stroke or other illness. Smallwood said they chose the project "because it was dealing with humans."

The big advantage to their device is that it is mobile, Smallwood said. Other rehabilitation techniques, such as hydrotherapy, require the patient to be in the water or walk in circles around a machine such as the Rehabot, which has a "dehumanizing" effect, Smallwood said.

Smallwood and Bonnstetter's device has the added advantage of being more affordable than the Rehabot, with the prototype costing about $1,300.

Khan and Wallace's project focused on producing lower-cost alternatives as well. Electric four-wheel steering systems are already used for big cars, Khan said, but they are too expensive for a compact car. "Ours was purely hydraulic, so it was cheaper," he said.

Khan, who will receive his master's in mechanical engineering in June, said Ford is interested in four-wheel steering because it is "easier for parking and it improves safety and stability of the car at high speeds." He said that "if you go into a skid, it provides more traction."

Several other students won Bronze and Merit awards.

The contest, which has sponsoring corporations, which including Apple, McDonnell Douglas Corp., Lockheed and others, pose a design problem to the students, who rank their preference of projects.

"The problem is a pertinent design problem they have, and they are giving students a crack at it," Twiss said.

The students work in teams of two or three people coached by a graduate student or industry volunteer.

"One thing that's gratifying about Prof. Leifer's class is that you can take an idea, conceptualize it, and finally come up with a working product," Twiss said.

In addition to the prizes won by students, Stanford was awarded $2,250, which, according to administrative assistant Kristin Anderson, will go back into the program for "lab upkeep or new computers or something to benefit the class."

Twiss said he'd "like to say I used the prize money for altruistic purposes, but if the truth be known I bought a CD player."

Kreig Ecklund
ME310 student, AY1991; teaching assistant, AY1992

> The lessons I learned about the design process, collaborative design and just how to manage time to achieve results are invaluable and continue to serve me today as I lead teams of engineers in designing radiotherapy treatment devices.

I took ME210 during the 1991–92 school year while Larry Leifer was on sabbatical and Bernie Roth led the class, along with a visiting professor from Australia named David Radcliffe. The next year, I was a Teaching Assistant along with Greg Twiss as Prof. Leifer taught the class once again, with the help of some grad students, Ade Mabogunje and Margot Brereton.

The art of early prototyping with low fidelity and continuing to increase the fidelity as the design matures has been particularly useful. I am sometimes amazed that even seasoned engineers I work with don't seem to understand some of the lessons I learned in ME210 a few decades ago!

I recall Prof. Roth and his refusal to accept excuses from classmates. If one said they didn't have time, he'd point out that they had the same amount of time as everyone else. If one complained that they didn't have sufficient budget to do something, he'd ask what else they could have done for which they did have funds. I learned so much from the interactions between myself, classmates, and Prof. Roth in terms of taking responsibility for myself, my time, and my work.

I remember Prof. Leifer as an incredibly open and perceptive teacher. His encouragement for students to try new things and explore was refreshing and liberating. In a setting full of high achievers who had rarely failed at anything, he encouraged trying new things and 'failing early to succeed sooner!'

I recall the ME210 community as being close knit and a lot of fun! The loft always had people in it, working or otherwise. The social functions and presentations knit the class together into a wonderful shared experience that transcended a mere academic class.

In my career, I have been involved in many different kinds of work from mechanical engineering to finance to information technology and medical device design. The lessons learned in ME210 have served me well in each and every endeavor, for all of them required design thinking, design process and collaboration. I am forever thankful for the head start I received by learning the lessons of ME210 early in my career!

Currently PMO Manager at Varian Medical Systems

Sami Bitar
ME310 student, AY1993; teaching assistant, AY1994

> It was a great fusion of design process theory but strongly grounded in a real-world project that forced us into doing a detailed design after completing a detailed analysis to building an actual, fully-functioning hardware prototype.

As an ME210 student in 1993–94, I got to work on a true mechatronics project on behalf of Boeing Company, whom working for had been a dream of mine since I was a child. The ME210 design loft was a tremendously open environment, both physically and in terms of intra- and inter-team dynamics.

From the exciting beginning of the year with the paper bike contest that was a most humbling and exciting event, to watching Larry Leifer in action wow the captains of industry during the end-of-year Design EXPE, observing Larry's leadership was quite a sight — his charm, and clear passion for technology and concurrent insistence on the more human and social aspects of design — were noteworthy then and as relevant today as they were almost 25 years ago.

The following year, I was an ME210 TA [*Teaching Assistant — editor*] in AY1994, and I have to say that this was a truly formative experience for me. I remember vividly that Larry was so open and considered his TAs so essential to the teaching staff that he literally gave us the keys to his office for us to use. From fundraising, to project management, to evaluating presentations, to honing and coaching communication skills, being an ME210 TA turned out to be great preparation for engineering management and for entrepreneurship which ended up being the career path I pursued. It's amazing and great that ME210 has made it to 50 years, and I wish the ME210 community all the best for another five decades to come.

Currently President and Co-Founder at MagCanica Inc.

Maria Yang, Ph.D.
ME310 observer, AY1992–AY1999

I knew about ME310 because my friends and my sister took and TA'd [*served as a Teaching Assistant — editor*] the course, and also because I was in CDR [*Stanford Center for Design Research — editor*] and many of the researchers engaged with the class.

ME210/310 has always been ahead of its time. Early on, it recognized the importance of the process of design in achieving innovative design outcomes. It embraced the value of the social aspects of team interactions in design. It also fearlessly adopted cutting-edge technologies and strategies for design before most everyone else, from globally distributed teams to web-enabled video conferencing to digital design notebooks. Not only did this approach lead to better learning, but it inspired students to become forward-thinking practitioners who push boundaries to make better futures possible through design.

ME310's impacts have gone beyond the classroom to the laboratory. It took the novel view that the classroom was a natural testbed environment for studying the early stages of the design process itself. The 'instrumented classroom' approach has allowed the design process to be captured and analyzed in rich detail in ways not possible in a typical experiment. This approach spurred a generation of design researchers, including myself, to think about the act of designing and design research in an expansive new way.

Currently Associate Professor of Mechanical Engineering at MIT

Sam Yen, Ph.D.
ME310 student, AY1996

I can share a word about being a student of ME210 (before it changed to ME310) in 1996. It was the first design class I took at Stanford and completely pivoted my education from aerospace engineering to design. I switched my masters in aero-astro and did my Ph.D. with Larry Leifer in CDR. I've since spent much of my career advocating design thinking from startup companies to the world's largest companies. I was also on the first geographically distributed team with a partner from Tokyo (Hideyuki Ando). This is common today in ME310, but back then, it was very challenging. This experience though has certainly helped in my career working in multinational companies.

Currently Head of Commercial Real Estate Digital at JP Morgan Chase & Co

Jesse Adams
ME310 student, AY1997

ME310 was a game changer for me. I remember the first day of class in the Truman building, September 1997. The real-world application of learning and learning through application on a very large scale came alive for me. Boundaries of past tradition in education and restrictions on charting new courses for development and learning were removed. Speaking of which, Larry Leifer also helped me chart a new course for the Ph.D. program in 2001. I carried much of this momentum into my professorship at University of Nevada, Reno (UNR), applying lessons and methods learned at Stanford to my classes (ME150 and ME452) at UNR. In 2016, I was able to help coordinate and participate in the ME310 project sponsored by Shoe INN, including a trip to Finland and seeing the Northern Lights! :) The innovation inspiration is still running strong, and I've recently created the fastest innovation accelerator we can imagine with a group of motivated friends and colleagues at corcom.io.

Thank you ME310, Larry, and team!!

Currently CEO at CorCom Matrix

Gabriel Aldaz, Ph.D., & Alex Asseily
ME310 students, AY1997

> Looking back, I am certain that ME210 set me on a career path in engineering consulting. The class taught me teamwork, both on the Stanford team and working with corporate clients.

The students of ME210 in 1997–98 were thrilled to learn that a corporate sponsor had made a new automobile available for a project. BMW offered a 525i as a testbed for students to design and prototype new interactions between car and driver. My team was fortunate to get the keys to the 525i, as many teams had ranked BMW as their first-choice corporate sponsor. Noah Brinton, Alex Asseily, Craig Litherland, and I worked tirelessly from the start on ambitious plans. We soon found out how challenging it was to implement anything in a working vehicle and were constantly behind the class deadlines. At one intermediate checkpoint where nothing was working, Larry Leifer famously asked, 'Is this a no-show? Do we have a no-show?'

During winter quarter, we accumulated an impressive collection of parking tickets. At last, we were granted permission to leave the 525i under a tent in the PRL patio. There we worked day and night, regularly making early morning runs to Chuck's Donuts in Woodside. In a time-honored tradition, we put the finishing touches on our demo a few minutes before our scheduled final presentation slot.

It's fun to recall the features we built into that 525i — futuristic then in 1998 — that are now commonplace in vehicles. For example, the doors unlocked when a person possessing our custom key fob reached for a door handle. The engine started when a person, detected in the driver's seat, pressed the start button (on the shift lever rather than the dashboard, as is common today). We even tried our luck at rudimentary voice detection. The command 'open trunk' would unlatch the trunk so it could spring open.

At the final presentation, a crowd gathered around the BMW to witness the demo. Alex, our spokesman, showed off the various features of the car. At last, he said 'open trunk!' — and nothing happened. That morning, Alex had made a desperate visit to Oki Semiconductor to repair the speech recognition system. They had apparently fixed the problem, but maybe not. After only a second of panic, he pointed to the key fob. 'It's in valet mode,' he announced. We had forgotten that we had built in a mode for valet parking, which disabled most of the functionality. When Alex put the key fob back in regular mode and commanded the trunk to open, it responded perfectly, and the crowd cheered.

Our BMW liaisons were Martin Wegge, Michael Koblbauer, and Paul Aschauer in Munich. Our team also employed a handful of consultants — one to design the key fob printed circuit board and a couple more to help with programming. And of course, we benefitted immensely from the guidance of Larry Leifer and Mark Cutkosky, who have made the class what it is today.

Gabriel is currently Director of the Bay Area Office at Simplexity Product Development

Alex is currently Founder at Zulu Group

Craig Litherland
ME310 student, AY1997

'All design is redesign' is one of Larry Leifer's mottos that I took from ME210 and have used throughout my adventures in R&D. I entered the class thinking it would be a great complement to my technical background in aerospace engineering, and it was. I also thought it might be fun and easy. I was right about the former, but not so much the latter. I think I did more all-nighters in ME210 than in my entire undergrad program.

'It's never too late to plan' was another lesson for me. BMW provided our team with a car that was fully functional — at least until we got to it. One night at 3 AM on the night before a major class demo, I accidentally shorted a wire and disabled the entire car. My team rallied, got on the phone with our partners in Germany (the time difference helped us this time), and figured out a solution by morning. The many successes and failures in the class helped us to forge the grit and wherewithal to tackle tough problems.

Here's to another 50 years of ME310. Nobody knows what problems and technologies students will be faced with in the future, but two things are for sure: it will always be difficult to build things, and it will always require a team.

Currently Chief Technology Officer and Co-Founder at eyeThera

Anne Flatté
ME310 videographer, AY1996

Professor Larry Leifer was a big source of energy behind the video documentary. It was a great project, and all the teams and individuals were wonderful to film.

Currently Director and Producer at Owsley Brown Presents

Description on back of video cassette:

Product-Based Learning (PBL) is an innovative active-learning teaching methodology which could revolutionize higher education. Professor Larry Leifer's PBL framwork has emerged from over a decade of teaching, testing and research in collaborative design. A key element of his work has been ME210: Team-Based Design-Development with Corporate Partners, a graduate course offered by the Mechanical Engineering Department at Stanford University. The class addresses crucial issues in engineering and design that have long been ignored in traditional education and industry, and prepares students to be successful leaders in today's global workplace. Unlike technical content which quickly becomes outdated, the skills and knowledge students acquire in ME210 form an enduring, living foundation that will last through their entire careers. By presenting a PBL environment in action, the video provides faculty with a model of this teaching methodology and students with an engaging preview of the PBL learning experience.

Lawrence Neeley, Ph.D.
ME310 student, AY1998

Since I've left Stanford, I've taught design at MIT as a post-doc and now at Olin as an associate professor. What has struck me as most amazing is how far ahead of its time ME310 was. Project-based and problem-based learning, real-world projects, for real clients with real impact and implications, teams with interdisciplinary abilities and skills, and distributed and global teams and collaboration… all of these practices and ideas that ME310 has embodied for decades are the innovations that many have only recently embraced. ME310 has been a constant source of innovation and inspiration, not just in the creative output of its students but in the conception, design, and implementation — and of the course itself.

Currently Associate Professor of Design & Entrepreneurship at Olin College of Engineering

2000s

The 2000s started with John Hennessy as Stanford's tenth president and the foothills surrounding "the Dish" becoming a habitat conservation area. Notable events included the dotcom bust in 2000, the 9/11 terrorist attack on American soil in 2001 and related U.S. "war on terror" in the Middle East, the euro entering circulation in 2002, a global outbreak of severe acute respiratory syndrome (SARS) in 2002–2003 and H1N1 (swine flu) pandemic in 2009, and a global economic crisis in 2007–2008. Offshore outsourcing grew. The Airbus A380 and Boeing 787 Dreamliner planes began production, and the Spirit rover landed on Mars in 2004. Social networking also exploded this decade. — *Editor*

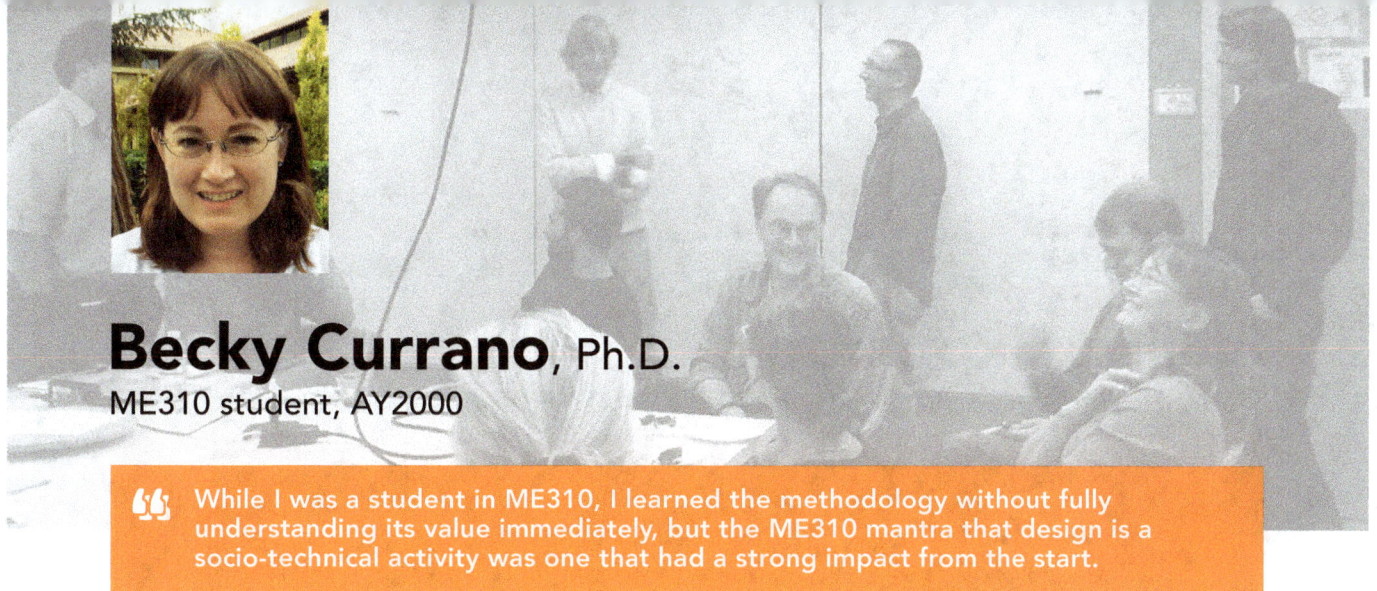

Becky Currano, Ph.D.
ME310 student, AY2000

> While I was a student in ME310, I learned the methodology without fully understanding its value immediately, but the ME310 mantra that design is a socio-technical activity was one that had a strong impact from the start.

An emphasis on building team bonds through a class day-trip at the beginning and end of the year, an early autumn team building excursion, budget allowances for decoration of team spaces, and of course, weekly SUDS [*Slightly Unorganized Design Session — editor*] dinners, not only fostered cohesion within our teams, but also provided frequent opportunity to mix with other teams and make new friends. Also, requirements to attend other teams' SGMs [*Small Group Meetings — editor*] from time to time, and student-led just-in-time tutorials, which took the place of regular lectures at the time, encouraged students to learn from each other, asking for help when needed, and sharing skills we learned with our classmates.

All of this is a lifesaver for first-year graduate students, especially those living off campus, who don't yet have a home community in the university. I am pretty sure the impact on my class' culture was uniquely strong, as we not only took other classes together, but we went out to dinner and karaoke regularly (across ME310 teams), took ski trips together, and even hosted our own ME310-themed pop music concert toward the end of the year. I believe these practices helped to ensure that the unavoidable conflicts that happen when working in teams did not cause lasting rifts within or between teams. And certainly they helped produce lasting friendships between many students.

Some of the more technical lessons and finer points of the ME310 methodology, such as an appreciation for early-stage ambiguity in the design process, and distinctions between design requirements and specifications, did not fully gel for me until after I had completed the course. But opportunities to coach the course in following years encouraged me to reflect on my own experience, helped to solidify these concepts, and were invaluable experiences in growing as a designer myself. ME310 definitely changed my understanding of design and the factors that enable designers and teams to produce more innovative outcomes. It was probably the most impactful course I participated in at Stanford.

Currently a Postdoctoral Scholar at the Center for Design Research at Stanford University

Philipp Skogstad, Ph.D.
Student, AY2003; T.A., AY2004; dir., AY2007–AY'09; sponsor, AY2010–AY'16

> I have seen ME310 from many perspectives: as student, course assistant, remote faculty, executive director, corporate liaison, and corporate executive.

I first joined the ME310 family in 2003 as a first-year graduate student, and this class has changed my life and career path more than any other class: 15 years later, 2 of my 3 closest friends are ME310 classmates, five of us from that class still hang out together regularly, and all have daughters who were born within 12 months of each other. Professionally, the class put me on track for a management career that has led me to my dream job — I learned the required tolerance for ambiguity and appreciation of failure in ME310.

In all my roles, I still see the same core: an opportunity for students to create their first start-up with a garage space, seed funding, an advisory board, and a first customer. This is an unparalleled opportunity for students and very consistent over the years. The value proposition for companies has also remained consistent as an opportunity to join an innovation community and a window into the technology trends that are important to the trend-setting customer segment.

ME310 has inspired countless faculty and students at Stanford and around the world, and as a result, its teaching model has become widespread 'commodity'. This is the typical evolution of any successful technology and business model. With my outside perspective now, I probably see the signs of danger more clearly than those on the inside or new to the family. I therefore challenge the Stanford faculty to go back to the question of what started ME310: 'What skill or experience is needed in today's world and not taught anywhere else?' Over time, it was mechatronics, global collaboration, project management, user experience, iteration — what is it now?

Currently President and CFO at Mercedes-Benz Research & Development North America Inc.

Neeraj Sonalkar, Ph.D.
ME310 student, AY2004

> That's one key thing about ME310 — learning and doing occurred simultaneously. And how much you got out of the class depended solely on how much you put in — both in action and reflection.

I took ME310 in my first year and first quarter of grad school. It was a weird class for me, coming right off the plane from Mumbai, India. The instructors, Larry Leifer and Mark Cutkosky, gave us some process guidelines, but did not teach any content. There was not much math involved. Instead of problem sets, we made prototypes, which mostly looked crappy. And there was some documentation involved with presentations, but no exams. This took some getting used to. And at the same time, it felt liberating. I was free to pursue curiosities and make things. I got to work in multiple teams and make unheard-of prototypes, which was a lot of fun! And the community of 310ers and the Stanford Design Group provided social support and made for a rich learning environment.

The 310 experience has been my archetype for what a learning experience could be. It prompted me to work with Larry Leifer to pursue research in engineering design. I studied 310 teams to develop a visual notation for characterizing team dynamics, which is now a team diagnostic that we are using with corporate and startup teams. And the broader community of ME310 made me realize the importance of having an ecosystem surrounding any design activity. This has led my colleagues and myself at the Center for Design Research to focus on not just design activity, but the development of regional innovation ecosystems. ME310 was the benchmark for us when we set out to develop learning and innovation environments in Nigeria and India.

Over the years, I have realized that 310 does have a dark side to it. I have met many students who were frustrated with their teams. Some left the course midway, and others wondered what they got out of it. In some ways, you need to be ready to take ME310… it's not any other class you just sign up for and coast through. A lot depends on the capability and emotional maturity of the student. The teaching team is always on hand to guide, but a lot depends on the student. She is the learner and the doer. In many ways, 310 is rehab for the consumer culture of education that we are socialized in as students! ME310 is a wonderful example of what engineering design learning could be and should be.

Currently Executive Director of Human Innovation Design Research at the Center for Design Research at Stanford University

Sushi Suzuki
ME310 student, AY2004; T.A., AY2005; executive director, AY2008

> Of all the things I've learned from being part of ME310 and SUGAR, of all the conversations I've had with Larry Leifer, the one clear message I take away is, 'You have to let people innovate.'

Taking ME310 was not my first choice when I arrived at Stanford in 2004. It was only because of scheduling that I decided to postpone another big project-based course until the second year and instead join ME310, a course I was mildly interested in. Looking back, I can't imagine how different my life would be if that scheduling conflict didn't exist. I never took that other course.

ME310 in 2004 was when the global element was just starting to take off. Not all projects had global teammates, and for the projects that did, there was no formal structure. For our project with BMW, our partners from the Technical University of Munich did not join the project until mid-January, nearly three months into the project, and we did not meet face-to-face until spring break. I don't think our German teammates knew what they were getting themselves into, and we kept sending all the assignments and milestones to keep them up to date. Nevertheless, they were some of the coolest people on the planet and great teammates to work with. Our project output would not have been the same without them for sure.

The following year, I became a teaching assistant for the course, and this was the first year Aalto University joined the program and the first time I met Lauri Repokari (his name will come up later). While there were other global projects, I distinctly remember the Panasonic team where three really powerful Finnish ladies from Aalto took the reins and led the project to a fascinating result (the Stanford students were quiet and unconfident throughout the entire project). This was the first time I've seen the power of Finnish culture.

I then left ME310 for almost two years as I joined Daimler-Chrysler in Silicon Valley, got kicked out of the U.S. because of a visa mishap, backpacked around South America, and then came back to replace Philipp Skogstad as ME310 executive director in 2008. By this point, every project in ME310 was globally distributed and there was much more structure around the collaboration, such as the kickoff workshop. As a result, fewer teams were getting 'divorced' during the project.

In 2009, I joined Veronique Hillen to bring ME310 to France and create a new design thinking program in Paris. That year we had one project with Stanford but wanted to expand the program so we reached out to Lauri Repokari at Aalto University. Being the always deviant optimist, he said yes without blinking, and the first non-Stanford global projects in ME310 were born (the term SUGAR did not exist yet). The same year, Aalto University had an extra project from a Finnish welding company that did not have a partner university. Instead of giving up on the project or running it locally, Lauri Repokari took an exchange student from Japan and asked if he could assemble a team in Japan. The student, whose home institution was the Kyoto Institute of Technology, called on his friends and in a week put together a team to join the project, without any professor in Japan knowing about it. That's how ME310 and SUGAR arrived in Kyoto, my hometown.

Fast forward several years and a stint back in industry, I am now teaching and coordinating ME310/SUGAR at the Kyoto Institute of Technology, and SUGAR has now grown to 30+ projects in 20+ universities on five continents. What started as an idea for a globally distributed design project has now become an international movement encompassing hundreds of people every year.

And you know what's amazing? Nobody asked for any permission.

The growth and spread of ME310 and SUGAR around the world has been incredibly organic, with passionate educators fighting bureaucracies and negotiating with companies to bring the program to their own country. No one was told to start their own ME310 program. I don't believe it was anybody's intent to have the program reach the corners of the world. But by creating the best possible design education program, and by letting people join, we now have the world's most intense global design program.

This is not to say that there were no growing pains. Scaling a program from a couple dozen students to hundreds can wreak havoc on infrastructure and resources. Coordination becomes increasingly difficult with more people. The challenges that companies experience when growing from a startup to an SME can be felt in ME310 and SUGAR as well.

Nevertheless, every time I meet my colleagues in California or around the world, every time I see the students proudly present their projects, and every time I catch up with an old alumnus, I feel the passion that has kept me going for so long. I do not know what will happen to ME310 or where SUGAR will go next, but it's been an amazing ride so far, and I'm glad I'm still getting to ride the waves with everyone.

Currently Associate Professor of Design Methodology and Mechanical Engineering at Kyoto Institute of Technology

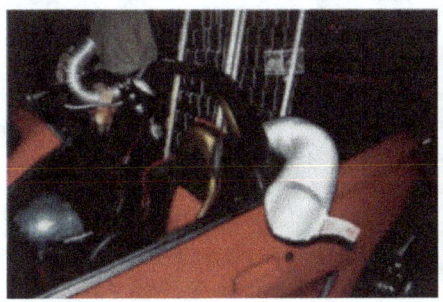

Mark Bianco
ME310 student, AY2005; coach, AY2006–AY2014

ME310 was a phenomenal experience for me. I'm sure that it has been the foundation for the careers of many successful engineers and entrepreneurs for the past half century, and a significant factor in making Silicon Valley the innovation epicenter that it is today.

Currently Manager in Mechanical Engineering in the Autonomous Driving Group at Intel Corporation

Micah Lande, Ph.D.
ME310 student, AY2005; teaching assistant, AY2006–AY2007

With the range of voices from the teaching team, how one responds directly to the perspectives of Larry Leifer, Mark Cutkosky, Vic Scheinman, and / or George Toye for their project direction is so interesting. And differing world views within the teaching team make impact in varying proportions, so what ratio forged your own unique engineering design approach? How much are you a Larry or Mark or Vic / George?

Currently Assistant Professor and E.R. Stensaas Chair for Engineering Education at South Dakota School of Mines and Technology

Dan Manian
ME310 student, AY2006; teaching assistant, AY2007

ME310 was a foundational experience for how to build and lead teams that create delightful, innovative products. From how to approach rapid prototyping and testing to collaborating with global teams, ME310 was one of the most hands-on, impactful, and transformative educational experiences I've had, both as a student and TA [*Teaching Assistant — editor*]!

Currently Co-Founder and CEO at Donut

Santhi (Elayaperumal) Analytis, Ph.D.
ME310 student, AY2007

I have had many amazing experiences through ME310. Some of my closest friends from grad school I met through the class and the network. From building a paper bike, hosting global partners, traveling internationally, and building prototypes, I have gained invaluable skills from the course which I honed during my Ph.D. research and while forming my company after graduating.

Recently CTO and Co-Founder at Moxxly

Jackie (Bernstein) Bernhelm
ME310 student, AY2007

ME310 taught me lessons that I use to this day in my career — how to embrace risk, how to connect with a global team, how to do instead of just think. Our team worked on a project targeted at getting teens to take more photos. At the time, cell phones had not yet replaced digital cameras, and our project sponsor Kodak was concerned that teenagers were going to take pictures differently than their parents. I'm really proud that our team identified the idea of a selfie a few years before they were a mainstream concept and designed a solution around this use case. Typical of a team of engineers, we overbuilt the concept and instead of pursuing our early selfie-stick prototype, we built a system that allowed your phone to take over a camera to take a remote picture. From this experience, a lesson I carry with me is that the best solution can be the simplest one.

Currently Founder in Residence at Google

Lindsey Sunden
ME310 student, AY2007; teaching assistant, AY2008

I can admit that this is only course where I still distinctly remember the exact lessons as taught — perhaps because I find myself repeating and reusing so many elements of the class in my work now. That designers preserve ambiguity. Fail often, and early. Prototype, prototype, prototype.

Professors Larry Leifer and Mark Cutkosky, and the entire teaching team, gave me the skill-set to comfortably navigate a world of filled with ill-defined problems — and more, to enjoy exploring them. ME310 was certainly the start of a path for me, beginning with the course, then becoming a TA [*teaching assistant — editor*], then working with other ME310 students at a company, and now, a few companies later, advising and coaching ME310 project teams using the same principles.

I certainly owe a huge thank you to the course, and I look forward to seeing many more years ahead for ME310.

Currently Director of Research in Mechanical Engineering at Fitbit

Miika Heikkinen
ME310 student, AY2007

> This course changed my life. Plain and simple it really did. I was an aspiring designer from Finland with a vague dream about becoming a car designer one day with no idea on how to make the dream happen.

My ME310 journey started quite randomly in Finland; one afternoon I walked into the office of the head of Industrial Design at Lahti to talk about my degree project and was told about this crazy email from Lauri Repokari he had just received which asked if there was anyone interested to apply for a course at Stanford and would be willing to move to California the following week. I applied instantly, and after a few interviews and trips to the U.S. embassy found myself all packed and ready to go with three other students from Finland (Tytti-Lotta Ojala, Anders Häggman, and Heikki Juvonen). To what I had no idea, but it sounded like a great adventure.

We arrived at Palo Alto, California, just as the paper bike competition was about to start so we missed the first element of the course (mostly about team building) but had to find our feet pretty quickly as the course was in full speed.

During one of the first days, we got the privilege to meet the staff and tutors, and I quickly got the picture that the course was led by two really different and unique characters; Mark Cutkosky and Larry Leifer, both incredibly intelligent in their own style. Mark seemed to be the more engineering driven and pragmatic one, whereas Larry was the one who 'painted with the bigger brush' and was the heart of the course. They both seemed incredibly approachable and welcomed us to the ME310 family instantly. Larry had a way of inspiring people with his cool and relaxed somewhat 'surfer dude' aura while dropping in extremely precious insights on various topics. No matter what was going on in the sidelines, Larry never showed it and always had time to comment on things. He made sure everyone felt like they belonged to the ME310 family and kept the spirits high throughout the

course. At every milestone, Larry had a way of boosting the morale, and I think we all were driven into thinking that our projects would be awesome and game-changing. Mark steered us with his calm and rational way and made sure the concepts had technical merit while also being of great use when trying to figure out the more technical elements.

I could go into great details about our project for Cadillac we did but will try to sum it up as briefly as possible; our project was about simplifying the center stack of a Cadillac CTS car as the complexity was disturbing the users from their main task of driving (although the official brief stated something quite different). We ended up stripping the 80 odd controls away and creating a system which allowed the user to choose how much or how little content needed to be on show at one time.

Reflecting back to the year, I was uncertain about my own skills and always imagined everyone to be on a completely different level as I was. The creative, supporting and inspiring environment of ME310 allowed me to find my feet and confidence while also teaching me about the art of really working hard and pushing the concepts and content further. I was really lucky to be paired with Nicole Sampson as she was the one with the common sense but never shot any of the crazy ideas down before quickly prototyping them. Our overseas team from UNAM was great as well and the art of working with a remote team is something that I still benefit from in my everyday working life.

Currently, I run a design agency from Finland focusing on concept and vehicle design. The tools and learnings from the ME310 course still affect my daily work life, and the confidence that I found during that year has fueled my career. I also learned a few really golden quotes which I still often refer to when giving presentations:
– Happy people create happy concepts
– Fail often, fail early
– Do first and ask for forgiveness later
– Diamonds are created in pressure

Currently Founding Partner at Northern Works

Anders Häggman, Ph.D.
ME310 student, AY2007; teaching assistant, AY2009

> Instead of learning specific technical skills or formulas during ME310, I learned something much more important — a new way of thinking and designing. And in the process, I gained life-long friends.

My ME310 adventure began with 24 hours notice. I can't remember how I found out about the class, but I do remember having only 'until tomorrow' to decide whether to move half-way across the world. Despite having no idea how I would finance the year or where I was going to live, I had already made up my mind.

I had never met the other students from Finland (Miika, Heikki, and Tytti-Lotta), so we met up before flying out. After having met only once or twice, we decided it would be a good idea if we all lived together. I got my visa from the U.S. embassy the day before my flight, and off we went, full of excitement. I can still clearly remember arriving at the Caltrain station and walking along California Avenue dragging my suitcase with a broken wheel behind me — it continuously wanted to swerve left and right, but not go straight. We made the Coronet Motel our base-camp for about a week, sharing a run-down room between the four of us. We spent our days at the loft and evenings house-hunting. Eventually we found a terrific place on Grant Avenue, complete with a swimming pool for the full California experience. Those first few weeks were some of the most event-filled times of my life (and the coming months didn't slow down much either). It was a good introduction to Larry's 'dance with ambiguity'.

As Larry and Mark say, design is a social process — an essential part of the ME310 experience for me were my fellow students and mentors, many of whom I still keep in touch with. There are too many stories and experiences to recount, but one that always brings a smile to my face is the 'Dark Horse' prototype we did. It included heating up the water molecules in the ambient air, and for that, we drilled several holes in a microwave and added some tubes to direct air in and out.

I remember our neighbouring teams were not entirely amused by the appearance of a buzzing microwave (with some safety features bypassed) appearing on the adjacent table. To complete the experience, we made tin foil hats that we wore as 'protection'. Eventually it didn't amount to much more than a fun memory and a step along our design and redesign journey. Creating my first 'Dark Horse' prototype was a liberating experience; I enjoyed the freedom to try wild

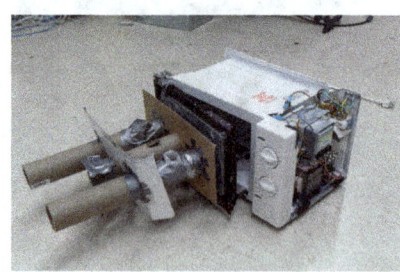

ideas — an experience I have recreated during my design career afterwards. During ME310, I learned to question assumptions and to search for the right questions to answer instead of grabbing onto the first solution.

The year I took ME310 was a life-changing experience for me, and it is hard to imagine where I would be now had I not taken the class ten years ago.

One of the main takeaways was realizing how limited my thinking had been and that I had in some ways held myself back; after the course I gained the courage to try and have not looked back since.

After ME310, I spent almost a decade in the U.S. having some of the most amazing experiences of my life (which includes my time at Stanford). During that time, I gained three wonderful daughters and graduated from MIT with a Ph.D. in design process, having done my thesis for Prof. Maria Yang, with fellow ME310 alum Prof. Warren Seering on my committee.

Even to this day, every time I think of ME310 I am filled with an overwhelming sense of gratitude for the opportunity that Larry, Mark, and Lauri Repokari gave me and to everyone else who made ME310 possible.

Currently Design Strategist at Protoomo and Research Affiliate at the Massachusetts Institute of Technology

Josh Carter
ME310 student, AY2008; teaching assistant, AY2009

As a decade removed from the program, one of the things that I find most compelling as I reflect on the experience is the intention brought to encouraging students to slow down and make space. The highly-driven, hyper-intelligent student that frequents Stanford Engineering programs is so often in a hurry to expand her skills and exercise his potential that neither values time and space. I was one of them, constantly pushing to work harder and smarter.

As I reflect on the 'Larry-isms' that have stuck with me most prominently, there's a common theme in creating space for the unexpected insights, immersing yourself in the journey of understanding your customer, and 'dancing with ambiguity'. There's something to that notion, and the program taught me to hear the 'beauty' in 'ambiguity', to run toward and embrace it, and in doing so to unlock great perspective and innovation for both myself as the designer and a given project at hand.

While I don't remember many specific skills that I learned from my time at Stanford, I remember the perspective I gained. The value of the resume I built through Stanford faded quickly, but the value of the mindset I built there is something I leverage every day. Those are the developments made during Stanford that I most cherish, and they're why I believe the ME310 program has been so impactful to its countless successful alumni. Thank you to the entire team and program and congratulations on 50 years of inspiration!

Currently Co-Founder & CEO at Aperia Technologies

Brandon Richardson
ME310 student, AY2008

ME310 was an amazing opportunity and was why I chose Stanford over other schools. Through ME310, not only did I gain an understanding of just how far I could push myself within a project (remember those 100+hr weeks before EXPE?), but I also gained a strong appreciation for the role of play and whimsy in the design process. I came from a 'hard' engineering background (I spent significant time in the automotive industry prior to grad school), and it was ME310 that helped me to re-align my values in order to cultivate a real spirit of innovation — both within myself, and for those around me. I would not be where I am today without having gone through ME310!

Currently Co-Founder & CTO at Aperia Technologies

Bryan Duggan
ME310 student, AY2008; teaching assistant, AY2009

> I witnessed some incredible products during my time with ME310, and it's amazing how many real-world products I've seen that are very similar to the solutions developed by ME310 teams over 5 years earlier.

I took ME310 because I felt like I needed to change my perspective on how products should be developed. I had been working in an advanced product development group for an automotive supplier, but most of the projects felt like incremental improvements, and real innovations were rare. Taking ME310 helped me find a better way to understand how to emphatize with user needs and to deliver product experiences that are useful and impactful. The focus on prototyping and testing pushed me to develop skills I had never used that are now part of my workflow every day.

TA'ing [serving as a Teaching Assistant — editor] ME310 provided possibly an even richer experience than taking the class as a student. Coaching the teams and seeing them explore and understand their problem spaces challenged me technically and creatively, and I really enjoyed learning from all of the students in the class. It was especially fulfilling to help them understand how to leverage the varied strengths (or mitigate weaknesses) of the individuals to build effective project teams.

I've also been extremely fortunate to be able to work with many ME310 alums since leaving Stanford. I've worked on numerous startups with friends from the class, and it's been so fulfilling and exciting to use the skills we gained to develop companies and products to solve important problems. No matter what the challenge, the people I've known from ME310 have been able to learn the skills or build the team necessary to do things no one has ever done before, and I don't believe I personally could have had the successes I've had without going through the class. I can say with certainty my experience with ME310 and everyone around it changed my life in ways I never imagined.

Currently Vice President of Product Management at Aperia Technologies

Chris Pell
ME310 student, AY2008

> Unlike other yearlong, project-based Mechanical Engineering classes, ME310 offers the opportunity to work with a cross-functional, internationally distributed team.

I was a part of the AY2008 ME310 class and worked on the project sponsored by Audi. This experience opened my eyes to both other disciplines of design / engineering and international perspectives. The projects require team members to see the bigger picture of product development and work outside the expertise they had developed in school.

ME310 carries with it a very entrepreneurial culture, and being immersed in it inspired me to pursue a summer program at Stanford's Graduate School of Business, then called the Summer Institute for Entrepreneurship (now Stanford Ignite). It was there that I met the co-founders of my first company. It is no surprise that many of my classmates and extended network from ME310 also went on to start companies.

My experience in ME310 taught me how design thinking can be widely applied. By having to work in a variety of domains, I became comfortable with not knowing the solution to a problem and gained confidence that I would be able to figure out new challenges. I have since worked as an independent consultant developing products for several companies in a wide variety of industries. Experiencing the broader view of product development and user-centered design also gave me the skills and confidence to be part of the formation of multiple startups since graduating.

I now try to pass the lessons I learned in ME310 onto my employees.

During my time in ME310, I also made some lifelong friendships both domestically and internationally.

Currently Director of Engineering at Luma Therapeutics

Mark Schar, Ph.D.
ME310 student, AY2008; ME310x faculty, AY2012–AY2013

> ❝ The course engages students with real problems that are ill-defined or improperly-defined, that have ambiguous and sometimes conflicting input, where there is no obvious path forward and asks these students to develop a successful solution.

ME310 is an important experience for the development of product management skills. This is what product management is all about and the skills developed in ME310 help insure that when these students face problems similar to these characteristics early or deep and within their careers they will have the confidence to move forward. Teaching ME310 also requires a special touch; being critical while encouraging, helpful without specific direction and patience while the student teams move forward toward a solution. Larry Leifer, Mark Cutkosky, and George Toye have formed a special teaching partnership that make this course possible.

For a period of years (2011–2016), we hosted a one-credit per quarter addition to ME310 called ME310X — the 'X' standing for 'experiential'. The course was a lecture/seminar format which provided the ME310 students with practical experience relating the various other disciplines they would encounter on a new product development team — finance, marketing, sales, public relations, legal. Each session was dedicated to one function and featured a 'hands-on' scenario, usually a case study example from business school and a guest speaker. Most guest speakers were classically trained engineers who had taken a lateral career move into another function, so they could relate to what the Stanford engineering students were learning while representing the role of their function they represented. The goal was to generate just enough familiarity with each discipline to make the students' transition into the role of product management more productive.

Currently Lecturer and Senior Researcher in Engineering at Stanford University

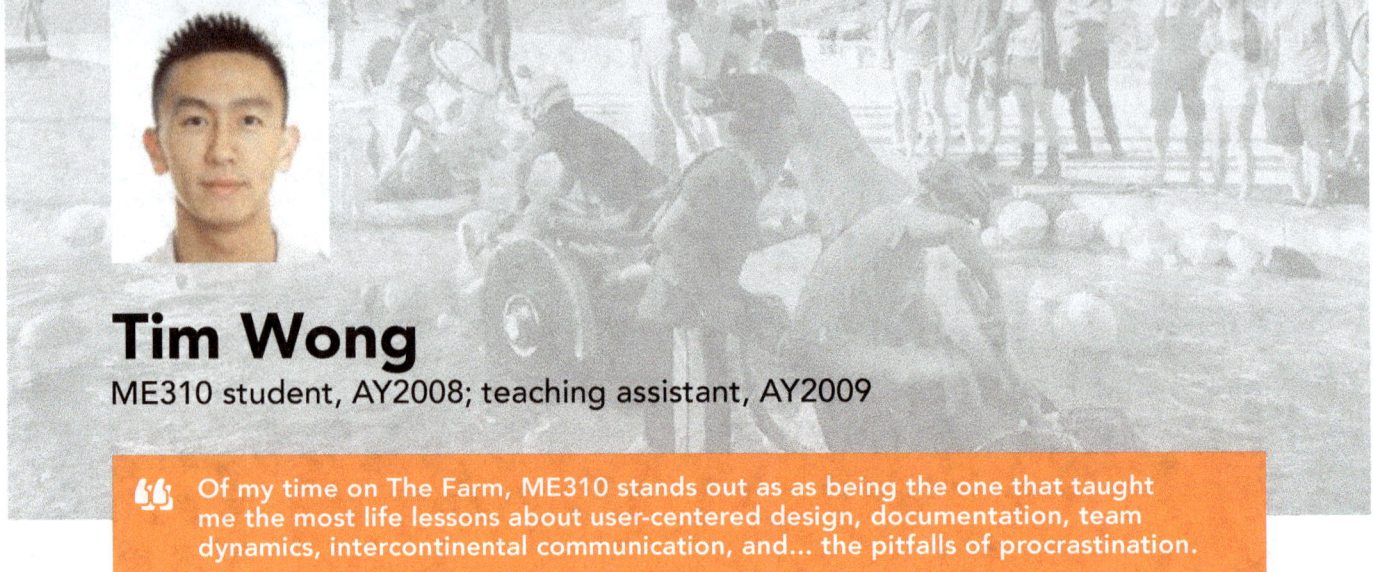

Tim Wong
ME310 student, AY2008; teaching assistant, AY2009

> Of my time on The Farm, ME310 stands out as as being the one that taught me the most life lessons about user-centered design, documentation, team dynamics, intercontinental communication, and… the pitfalls of procrastination.

As a Stanford MSME alumnus from eight years ago (2008–2010), one class still remains thoroughly embedded in my memory — ME310.

I have the fortune of having a unique perspective from both sides of the table — both as a student and serving on the T-Team. I could drone on about how each of these roles helped me develop skills I still use today (and they have!), but instead I'll choose to reminisce on a common thread that ran through not only my two years in the loft, but also one that has spanned a continuous stretch of ME310 generations through today: paper bike!

It's a class tradition that is as ridiculous as it sounds — building a 'bike' from nothing more than paper-based materials and is capable of not only transporting a passenger, but also to compete in a task-oriented game (while also getting pummeled with water balloons by bystanders). Oh, and do this with only about 2 weeks time on a team of people you've just met. While this may sound like a chaotic affair, and at times it is, looking at it from ten thousand feet will reveal that there is a surprising amount of process built into the exercise. It really takes you through an entire journey: from forming a team comprised of members with varying backgrounds, skill sets, and communication styles, brainstorming a million different ideas, selecting a few promising critical subsystems to prototype, designing and CAD, and then to actually building and documentation.

As a side note — in the process, through many late nights in the loft, I also happened to form a bond with a then-complete stranger. We later became corporate project teammates, great friends, and… many years later, each other's groomsmen! ME310 has been a gift that has continued to give.

Currently Mechanical Engineer at Trimble Navigation Ltd.

2010s

The 2010 decade began amid a world financial crisis. In 2011, Stanford earned its 100th NCAA team national title. In 2016, Stanford celebrated its 125th anniversary, and Marc Tessier-Lavigne became the university's 11th president. Outside Stanford, Apple iPad and the first quantum computing machine debuted in 2010, the Curiosity rover landed on Mars in 2012, and CRISPR genome editing occurred in 2013. Mobile devices and social networking became widespread, and app stores like Google and Apple grew in use. The decade also saw a rise in drones, 3D printing, virtual assistants, virtual reality headsets, smart watches, and e-cigarettes. Cyber-hacking and security threats grew, and crypto-currency like Bitcoin sparked wide interest. — *Editor*

Tyler Bushnell
ME310 student, AY2011; teaching assistant, AY2012

'OK, let's get started.' After everyone rolls, scoots, and slides their seats clanking into place, the team speaks loud enough that everyone can hear them over the background chatter of other teams preparing for their own SGMs [*Small Group Meetings — editor*]. They emphatically explain what brought them to this prototype and finish their speech, waiting for someone to voice their first question.

Larry Leifer leans forward slowly: 'I'm not sure I heard all of that, but how about this….' His feedback is adept. He taps into something fundamental and overlooked. There's so much to pay attention to in every interaction. Just listening to what people say can be misleading. That's ME310.

ME310 is a course that introduces you to the hard problems that are ambiguous, interpersonal, innovative, and still feasible. After the class, all problems seem solvable, and all solutions have alternatives. I'm able to use tools from the course whenever I'm working on new designs or trying to get people to consider new concepts.

Currently Product Designer at Apple

Alexandre Jais
ME310 student, AY2012

ME310 was the first time I heard about a class that taught empathy and being able to work with ambiguity; today it is impossible for me to do without those values in my work and personal life. Lacking those values cripples organizations and leaders in my opinion and experience, and it is very rare where one can get to experience them in a safe setting like ME310.

Currently CTO & Co-Founder at ETQ Labs

Tyler Bushnell
ME310 student, AY2011; teaching assistant, AY2012

'OK, let's get started.' After everyone rolls, scoots, and pushes their seats clanking into high gear, the team speaks loud enough that everyone can hear them over the background chatter of other teams preparing for their own SGMs [Small Group Meetings — editor]. They emphatically explain what brought them to this prototype and finish their speech, waiting for someone to voice their first question.

Larry Leifer leans forward slowly: 'I'm not sure I heard all of that, but how about this….' His feedback is adept. He taps into something fundamental and overlooked. There's so much to pay attention to in every interaction. Just listening to what people say can be misleading. That's ME310.

ME310 is a course that introduces you to the hard problems that are ambiguous, interpersonal, innovative, and still feasible. After the class, all problems seem solvable, and all solutions have alternatives. I'm able to use tools from the course whenever I'm working on new designs or trying to get people to consider new concepts.

Currently Product Designer at Apple

Alexandre Jais
ME310 student, AY2012

ME310 was the first time I heard about a class that taught empathy and being able to work with ambiguity; today it is impossible for me to do without those values in my work and personal life. Lacking those values cripples organizations and leaders in my opinion and experience, and it is very rare where one can get to experience them in a safe setting like ME310.

Currently CTO & Co-Founder at ETQ Labs

Tatiana Salazar
ME310 global student, AY2011

> More important than the 'how', which I attribute to the problem-based and in-real-context nature of the class, ME310 gave me the confidence that I was able to create solutions with real social innovation impact in a systematic way.

Growing up in a low-income family in Colombia, I never expected to receive a higher education. My mother did not finish high school, and my father barely graduated from community college. Fortunately, I was sponsored to study engineering at the Javeriana University in Colombia by a businessman who believes that education brings people out of poverty. My gratitude for his generosity evolved into one of my life goals — to help others access the quality higher-education I nearly missed. Although engineering school gave me a lot of tools to work towards that goal, I couldn't understand how to use them to produce real impact. ME310 taught me how to use those tools to solve complex problems.

I was overjoyed and humbled by the opportunity to join ME310 as part of the eight students who represented my Columbian university in the AY2011 class.

Our project's brief was to find a way for young people to engage with the brand of a traditional newspaper in Colombia. It was not an easy mission; the newspaper had been failing in reaching this market segment for years. People prematurely assumed that a successful solution involving young people would be completely digital. An intense process of thorough research, empathy, ideation, prototyping, and testing led us to an unexpected solution — a physical space where Colombian youth could interact with each other and browse/share relevant information using a web-based interface. This user-centered solution came from the discovery that young Colombians are strongly inclined towards face-to-face social interaction with their peers, which they find lacking in digital means of communication. After finishing the class, my team and I were extended a job offer to work with the newspaper to bring what we have learned about their target users, design thinking, and problem-solving skills to their company.

As tempting as their offer sounded to me, it was inevitable for me to fall in love not only with design but also with one of my Stanford classmates: Yong Lin. Yong and I share extremely similar backgrounds; although I grew up in Colombia and he in China, we both shared a passion for social justice, education, diversity, inclusion, and technology.

Almost two years after I met Yong at Stanford, I married him. Five years have passed since we said: 'I do'. In the years we have been together, we have been through lots of adventures from starting up with our friends a company in China that has helped thousands of students achieve their academic dreams of moving to Mountain View, California, and finally to working in our dream problem spaces. I am currently honored to be empowering learners around the globe as the design lead at Khan Academy.

I don't think it is an understatement to say that ME310 changed my life. It gave me the professional tools to make my social-centered goals a reality, it gave me the confidence to become a designer, and it gave me someone amazing to share my life with.

Currently Senior Product Designer at Khan Academy

Yong Lin
ME310 student, AY2011

ME310 is the most valuable course I had in my entire academic life. It has brought me the bravery to face ambiguity, the confidence to be creative, the perseverance to keep pushing forward when all the attempts to innovate fail, and a consistent way to achieve innovation. Personally, it also brought me the better half of myself — my wife. She was one of the team members of our international academic partner team from Colombia. Her intelligence, kindness, and passion ignited the love in my heart. We started dating in secret and kept a long-distance relationship. When I graduated from Stanford, we decided to get married and started a new life together in Silicon Valley.

Currently, we both work here in tech startups, and what we learned in ME310 has benefited us a lot in our work. Today I am the head of mobile development at Lark Technologies, which builds an AI health coaching chatbot to save people from chronic diseases. She is a lead product designer in Khan Academy. Design thinking has given us a way to keep innovating in the health and education industries.

Currently Head of Mobile at Lark Technologies

Teresa Tombelli
ME310 student, AY2014; teaching assistant, AY2015

> I think of ME310 as a prototype of a high pressure career. Students have freedom and accountability, but the stakes are lower — meaning there is room to try things and fail. While often hard to articulate, I think this environment is the most valuable.

Coming in as a grad student, most of my memories of Stanford are from ME310. I had already built my foundation in engineering at the University of Michigan, and I hoped that at Stanford I could cap my education with some great practical experience, and that it would propel me into a job in design engineering that I would enjoy. I chose 310 because it sounded like incredible fun, and because one final, serious project course would fit nicely with the other two that were already on my resume.

Luckily for me, 310 was a wonderful experience from start to finish. I was part of a team who genuinely enjoyed working together and motivated each other to take full advantage of every opportunity. Each of us was new to California, and we were still enjoying every drop of sunshine and the exhilarating freedom that 310 offered.

When you're in the thick of it, it's easy to take for granted all of the things that 310 offers to students. But to have almost unlimited control of your project direction, a generous budget from corporate sponsors, and weekly, personal support from three Stanford professors is something incredibly valuable that is not offered anywhere else.

For me, my 310 project was the first that I had done outside the academic vacuum, with hardware deliverables grounding the project in reality. The most valuable things I learned built on my engineering judgement — how to frame an open problem, manage ambiguity, collaborate with difficult people, and when to give up on an idea. These are all things that are critical to success on any real engineering project, and skills I use every day. I have found in my few years working at Microsoft that it's often these things that determine the success of a program, not engineering expertise.

I am so grateful that I had the chance to learn from ME310 as a student, and again in a different way as a teaching assistant. I still enjoy visiting the course, because 310 and the SUGAR network are always made up of amazing, bright, ambitious young people who make me feel optimistic about the future. I hope this class can continue inspiring students for another 50 years!

Currently Mechanical Engineer at Microsoft

The Extras

Course Listings

The course description for ME310 has changed over the years, as the teaching team has responded to industry trends, shifting student interest, and personal beliefs. A selection of ME310 course descriptions from the *Stanford University Bulletin* course catalog across the years is included here. In early years, the course title was often just "Engineering Design", but in later years, the course title emphasized other aspects of the learning experience in order to better appeal to students. ME is short for Mechanical Engineering, and courses in the 200–300 range are usually geared for masters' level students. And while credit units have ranged from 2 to 6 per quarter, most students would attest to an intense workload! — *Editor*

AY1968: ME219 A,B,C

ME219A. Advanced Engineering Design — Experience in the design of a machine. Technical requirements and interactions of various disciplines will be emphasized. The design will be carried through working drawings. Machine members will be fabricated from the drawings during Winter Quarter and the machine developed in 219C. This course and 219C constitute a series. The intent of the series is to involve the student in a major portion of the design-development process. Students should enroll for both courses. Grades will be deferred until the completion of 219C. Limited enrollment. Prerequisite: 114A or equivalent.
3 units, Aut (Adams) TTh 12:00-2:05

ME219B. Design Operations — Synopsis of operations common to many design projects followed by more detailed study of case histories of design projects from various environments. Planning the experimental development of a design produced in 219A or of an approved alternate. Prerequisite: consent of instructor.
3 units, Win (Fuchs) TTh 3:15-5:05

ME219C. Experimental Development Engineering — Testing and improvement of the design produced in 219A or approved alternate. Limited enrollment. Prerequisites: 219A or B, or consent of instructor.
2 units, Spr (Adams, Fuchs) lab. MW 1:15-4:05

AY1972: ME201 A,B,C

ME201A,B,C. Engineering Design — An intensive treatment of engineering design. The package will consist of project work accompanied by investigations of the design process and the study of material of particular value to the engineer involved in design activity. Projects will be carried through fabrication and testing. Special emphasis will be given to the conceptual and the development processes, information collection and organization, failure mode prediction, legal aspects of design, use of the computer and of mathematical analysis in design, protection of intellectual property, production considerations, interpersonal problems faced by the designer in various professional environments, design aesthetics, and man-machine integration. The course will be team-taught and will involve all Design Division faculty members. These three courses constitute an integrated series. Students wishing to enroll in a portion of the series must obtain the consent of the instructor. Prerequisite: graduate standing.
201 A. 6 units, Aut (Staff) TTh 1 -.15-4:05
201B. 6 units, Win (Staff) TTh 3:15-5:05 plus 1 hour by arrangement
201C. 6 units, Spr (Staff) MW1:15-4:05

COURSES AND DEGREES 1972–73
Stanford University Bulletin

AY1975: ME210 A,B,C

ME210 A,B,C. Engineering Design — Experience in the formulation, design and analysis of real engineering projects presented by local industry. Designs will be developed by small groups of students, each group under supervision of an instructor from the Design Division faculty and in close cooperation with the industrial sponsor. Projects will be carried through construction and testing of prototype, and first design revision. Instruction in design methodology, safety, liability, and patents for engineers. Students should enroll for all three courses. Grading will be deferred until completion of 210C. Limited enrollment. Prerequisite: 113 or equivalent.
210A. 4 units, Aut (Piziali, Liu) TTh 1:15-4:05
210B. 2 units, Win (Piziali, Liu) Th 2:15-5:05
210C. 3 units, Spr (Piziali, Liu) W 1:15-4:05

STANFORD UNIVERSITY BULLETIN

Courses and Degrees
1975-76

AY1979: ME210 A,B,C

ME210A,B,C. Engineering Design — Experience in the formulation, design and analysis of real engineering projects presented by local industry. Designs will be developed by small groups of students, each group under supervision of an instructor from the Design Division faculty and in close cooperation with the industrial sponsor. Projects will be carried through construction and testing of prototype, and first design revision. Instruction in design methodology, safety, liability, and patents for engineers. Students should enroll for all three courses. Grading will be deferred until completion of 210C. Limited enrollment. Prerequisite: 113 or equivalent.
210A. 4 units, Aut (Barkan, Staff) TTh 1:15-4:05
210B. 3 units, Win (Barkan, Staff) Th 2:15-5:05
210C. 3 units, Spr (Barkan, Staff) T 2:15-5:05

AY1982: ME210 A,B,C

ME210A,B,C. Engineering Design — Experience in the formulation, design and analysis of real engineering projects presented by industry. Designs will be developed by small groups of students, each group under supervision of an instructor from the Design Division faculty and in close cooperation with the industrial sponsor. Projects will be carried through construction and testing of prototype, and first design revision. Instruction in design methodology, safety, liability, and patents for engineers. Students should enroll for all three courses. Provides experience in technical presentations —both oral and written. Students unfamiliar with manufacturing process or drafting are encouraged to enroll also in 103 and 103D. Limited enrollment. Prerequisite: 113 or equivalent.
210A. 4 units, Aut (Chilton, Staff) TTh 3:15-5:05
210B. 3 units, Win (Chilton, Staff) Th 3:15-5:05
210C. 3 units, Spr (Chilton, Staff) W 3:15-5:05

AY1988: ME210 A,B,C

ME210A,B,C. Engineering Design — Experience in the formulation, design, and analysis of real engineering projects offered by industry. Design is developed and constructed through hardware phase by small groups of students under supervision of Design Division faculty and in close cooperation with the industrial sponsor. Some sponsored projects are manufacturing-oriented, and some offer opportunity for application of automation principles, microprocessors, controls, and sensors. Students with such interests should enroll in both 210 and 218. Projects are carried through construction and testing of a prototype, and first design revision. Instruction includes design methodology, design for manufacturability, project planning, safety, liability, and patenting. Students must enroll for all three courses. Experience in technical presentations, oral and written is stressed. Students unfamiliar with manufacturing processing or drafting are encouraged to enroll also in 103 and 103D. Limited enrollment. Prerequisite: 113 or equivalent.
210A. 4 units, Aut (Leifer, Staff) TTh 3:15-5:05
210B. 3 units, Win (Leifer, Staff) W 3:15-5:05
210C. 3 units, Spr (Leifer, Staff) Th 3:15-5:05

AY1992: ME210 A,B,C

ME210A. Automation and Machine Design: Methodology — Industry-sponsored projects develop the graduate engineer's knowledge of and skill applying structured concurrent engineering design methodology. Corporate representatives deliver project specific technology while the teaching team focuses on methodology. Three short design exercises sharpen student methods awareness and develop team design skills in preparation for the sponsored project. Following project selection, the design team refines the problem statement; develops detailed functional, physical, and constraint specifications; and identifies design approach alternatives, supported by a design coach, corporate liaison, and faculty advisers. Project content may include: mechanism design, automation design, manufacturing process design, consumer product, and biomedical device design. Students wishing to integrate microcomputer technology, sensors, and automatic control theory should enroll in both 210 and 218. Students may exit the 210 series only at the end of 210A.
4 units, Aut (Leifer) TTh 3:15-5:05

ME210B. Automation and Machine Design: Rapid Prototyping — Continuation of 210A. Design alternatives are subjected to rigorous examination by rapid prototyping and design trade-off analysis. Emphasis is on design for manufacturability, assembly, test, service, cost, and human factors. Incremental test/assessment development cycles are supported by the design lab's CAD, simulation, and physical prototyping facilities.
4 units, Win (Leifer) TTh 3:15-5:05

ME210C. Automation and Machine Design: Functional Assessment — Continuation of 210B. One or more leading design alternatives are developed into full-scale functional product prototypes. Emphasis on oral and written presentation skills prevails throughout 210C and climaxes at the Design Affiliates Symposium where projects are formally presented to an industrial audience.
4 units, Spr (Leifer) TTh 3:15-5:05

AY1996: ME210 A,B,C

ME210A. Experiences in Team-Based Design — First of three-quarter series. Design by immersion in a product development environment for interdisciplinary, distributed, engineering design-teams. Series of four design-development cycles, each with different team members and functional hardware outcomes, explore application of design theory and methodology to design practice. Work guided by case readings. May be taken alone, but required to continue to 210B,C. Enrollment limited and based on a statement of learning objectives due the second day of class.
4 units, Aut (Leifer)

ME210B. Team-Based Design-Development with Corporate Partners — (Continuation of 210A.) Following project selection, design team refines the problem statement; defines detailed functional, physical, and external requirements and develops the socio-technical infrastructure for self-management. Design teams are supported by a professional coach, corporate liaison, and faculty adviser. Corporate projects provide the technical content, motivation, and financial resources for a six-month long product development cycle. Design alternatives are subjected to rigorous examination by computational and physical simulation, trade-off analysis, and literature review. Manufacturability, assembly, test, service, life-cycle-cost, human factors and design for redesign are stressed. At least one design alternative is developed into a full-scale, functional, prototype. Limited enrollment. Prerequisite: 210A.
4 units, Win (Leifer)

ME210C. Team-Based Design-Development with Corporate Partners — (Continuation of 210B.) Final designs and function prototypes are presented to corporate sponsors at the Design Affiliates Conference the first week in June. Limited enrollment.
4 units, Spr (Leifer)

AY2001: ME310 A,B,C

ME310A. Tools for Team-Based Design — (Same as Engineering 310A.) For graduate students; open to limited SITN/global enrollment. Project based, exposing students to the tools and methodologies useful for forming and managing an effective engineering design team in a business environment, including product development teams that may be spread around the world. Topics: personality profiles for creating teams with balanced diversity; computational tools for project coordination and management; real time electronic documentation as a critical design process variable; methods for refining project requirements to ensure that the team addresses the right problem with the right solution. Computer-aided tools are employed for supporting geographically distributed teams. The final project analyzes a set of industry-sponsored design projects for consideration in 310B,C. The investigation includes benchmarking and meetings with industrial clients. The deliverable is a detailed document with specifications for the project and the optimal design team that should work on the project in subsequent quarters. Limited enrollment, consent of instructor for off campus (global) registrants.
4 units, Aut (Leifer)

ME310B,C. Design Project Experience with Corporate Partners — (Same as Engineering 310B,C.) Two-quarter project for graduate students who already have some design experience and want in-depth involvement in an entrepreneurial design team with real world industrial partners. The products developed are part of the student's portfolio. For some projects, 217 and 218 may be prerequisites or corequisites (see http://me310.stanford.edu for admission guidelines). Each team functions like a small startup company, working closely with a technical advisory board, consisting of the instructional staff and a coach. Teams use computer-aided tools for project management, communication, and documentation, and are provided a budget for direct expenses including hiring technical assistants and conducting tests. Teams interact with corporate liaisons weekly via site visits, video conferencing, email, fax, and phone. Hardware demonstrations, peer reviews, scheduled documentation releases, and an intense team environment provide the mechanisms and culture for design information sharing. Enrollment by consent of instructor and depends on the results of a pre-enrollment survey in December and the recommendations made by project definition teams in 310A.
4-5 units, Win, Spr (Leifer)

AY2008: ME310 A,B,C

ME310A. Project-Based Engineering Design, Innovation, and Development — Three quarter sequence; for engineering graduate students intending to lead projects related to sustainability, automotive, biomedical devices, communication, and user interaction. Student teams collaborate with academic partners in Europe, Asia, and Latin America on product innovation challenges presented by global corporations to design requirements and construct functional prototypes for consumer testing and technical evaluation. Design loft format such as found in Silicon Valley consultancies. Typically requires international travel. Prerequisites: undergraduate engineering design project; consent of instructor.
5 units, Aut (Leifer, L; Cutkosky, M)

ME310B. Project-Based Engineering Design, Innovation, and Development — (Same as ENGR 310B.) Three quarter sequence; for engineering graduate students intending to lead projects related to sustainability, automotive, biomedical devices, communication, and user interaction. Student teams collaborate with academic partners in Europe, Asia, and Latin America on product innovation challenges presented by global corporations to design requirements and construct functional prototypes for consumer testing and technical evaluation. Design loft format such as found in Silicon Valley consultancies. Typically requires international travel. Prerequisites: undergraduate engineering design project; consent of instructor.
5 units, Win (Leifer, L; Cutkosky, M)

ME310C. Project-Based Engineering Design, Innovation, and Development — Three quarter sequence; for engineering graduate students intending to lead projects related to sustainability, automotive, biomedical devices, communication, and user interaction. Student teams collaborate with academic partners in Europe, Asia, and Latin America on product innovation challenges presented by global corporations to design requirements and construct functional prototypes for consumer testing and technical evaluation. Design loft format such as found in Silicon Valley consultancies. Typically requires international travel. Prerequisites: undergraduate engineering design project; consent of instructor.
5 units, Spr (Leifer, L; Cutkosky, M)

Lexicon

ME310 has introduced multiple concepts and reserved terms, such as the dark horse prototype and SUDS, that have become an integral part of the student learning experience and design process. Some concepts have been lost over the years, while others have been adopted and adapted by ME310 global partners, informing engineering design teaching and practice worldwide. Incidentally, while some ME310 global partners describe the ME310 approach as "design thinking", it is typically not a part of ME310 class language. Instead, the founding team of Stanford's d.school drew inspiration from the greater engineering design community, including the ME310 legacy and close proximity to the ME310 loft. — *Editor*

Common Terms

Critical Experience prototype (CEP)
A Critical Experience prototype helps a design team see how a user might respond to some aspect or element of a proposed design. Ideally, this prototype is tested by people who are representative of the target users. It is not a prototype for a product but explores one possible direction.

Critical Functional prototype (CFP)
A Critical Functional prototype helps test an essential functional aspect or element underlying a design concept and helps a team to answer an important question about plausibility or feasibility. It is not a prototype for a product but explores one possible direction.

Dark Horse prototype
A Dark Horse prototype is a prototype that tests an idea or approach that the team had overlooked or earlier dismissed in their design process. In horse racing, the "dark horse" is the contender that unexpectedly comes from behind to win the race. A Dark Horse prototype could be an alternative to an earlier design concept, or it can focus on a different level of detail or a different target user.

EXPE
EXPE is the short name for the Design EXPErience, a year-end showcase organized by the Mechanical Engineering department's Design Group at Stanford University for their project-based courses. Historically, the ME310 course has presented the largest number of projects at EXPE each year.

Funky System prototype
A Funktional System or "Funky" prototype is one for which existing parts have been hacked and brought together in a manner that approximates a system without making a costly commitment to any one configuration, technology, or geometry. It is a low commitment, rapidly assembled, concept prototype that still allows for objective evaluation and testing. This prototype doesn't have to be pretty, but it should work.

Large Group Meeting (LGM)
A large group meeting, or LGM for short, refers to a design session with the entire ME310 class.

Mission
A class assignment is called a mission to convey a driving purpose for team learning.

Paper Bike Rally
The paper bike rally is an early team assignment to design, build, and race a functioning bicycle from cardboard, paper, and other non-metal components. This race has become an enduring team tradition, and competition rules change annually, often set by the ME310 teaching assistants.

Small Group Meeting (SGM)
A small group meeting, or SGM for short, refers to a design session with 2-3 ME310 project teams.

SUDS
SUDS is a weekly informal dinner for all ME310 students, in which project teams rotate dinner duties. SUDS is an acronym for Slightly Unorganized Design Session, and class alumni and other guests are often welcome.

Publications

The ME310 class has provided an ongoing data source for scholars at Stanford and other institutions. Especially since the 1980s, the ME310 teaching team has been involved with Stanford's Center for Design Research, which has further encouraged seeing ME310 as a mini laboratory to investigate a variety of topics — including project-based learning, the design process, team coaching, electronic notebooks, and prototyping. Here follows a partial list of research publications and other citations about the class as documented and/or studied across various sources, as well as several related references directly influenced by the ME310 body of work. The list is organized loosely by category. — *Editor*

General

Carleton, T., & Leifer, L.J. (2009). Stanford's ME310 course as an evolution of engineering design. Paper presented at the 19th CIRP Design Conference, Cranfield, United Kingdom.

Flatté, A. (Producer & Director). (1997). *ME210: An Experience in Product-Based Learning (VHS)*. United States: Stanford University.

Kubota, T. (2018, June 14). Stanford engineering design course reaches its 50th year. *Stanford News*.

Stanford University. (n.d.). Mechanical Engineering-310 digital collection (1976-2008). Available at https://purl.stanford.edu/md481fb4654

Stanford University. (n.d.). ME310 Project Based Engineering Design digital collection (2006-2018). Available at https://purl.stanford.edu/kq629sd5182

Problem-Based Learning

Berglund, A., Klasén, I., Hansson, M., & Grimheden, M. (2011). Changing mindsets, improving creativity and innovation in engineering education. *DS 69: Proceedings of E&PDE 2011, the 13th International Conference on Engineering and Product Design Education*, 121-126.

Leifer, L. (1995). Evaluating product-based-learning education. *Proceedings of the International Workshop on the Evaluation of Engineering Education*. Osaka, Japan.

Leifer, L. (1998). Design teaching: Beyond design education with product-based-learning, electronic-learning-portfolios and global teams. *Proceedings From Engineering Design Conference '98*: 11-20.

Steinbeck, R. (2011). Building creative competence in globally distributed courses through design thinking. *Revista Comunicar, XIX*(37): 27-34.

Taratukhin, V., & Pulyavina, N. (2018). The future of project-based learning for engineering and management students: Towards an advanced design thinking approach. Paper presented at the 2018 ASEE Annual Conference & Exposition, Salt Lake City, Utah.

Design Process

Baya, Vinod. (1996). *Information handling behavior of designers during conceptual design: Three experiments* (Unpublished doctoral dissertation). Stanford University, Stanford, CA.

Brereton, M., Sheppard, S., & Leifer, L. (1995). Students connecting engineering fundamentals and hardware design: Observations and implications for the design of curriculum and assessment methods. *Proceedings From 25th Annual Conference on Frontiers in Education - Engineering Education for the 21st-Century (IEEE 1995)*, 950-956.

Camacho, M. (2016) David Kelley: From design to design thinking at Stanford and IDEO. *She Ji: The Journal of Design, Economics, and Innovation, 2*(1): 88-101.

Eris, O. (2004). Effective Inquiry for Innovative Engineering Design (pp. 51-64). Boston, MA: Springer.

Häger, F., & Uflacker, M. (2016). Time management practice in educational design thinking projects. *DS 85-2: Proceedings of NordDesign 2016, 2*: 319-328.

Hutterer, P., Ozgur, E., Jung, M., Leifer, L.J., Lindemann, U., & Mabogunje, A. (2004). What do designers really need? An explorative experiment before developing teaching tools and methods. Paper presented at the IADIS (International Association for Development of the Information Society) Conference, Lisbon, Portugal.

Ju, W., Ionescu, A., Neeley, L., & Winograd, T. (2004). Where the wild things work: capturing shared physical design workspaces. *Proceedings of the 2004 ACM Conference on Computer Supported Cooperative Work (CSCW 2004)*, 533-541.

Leifer, L., Baya, V., Toye, G., Baudin, C., & Underwood, J.G. (1994). Engineering design knowledge recycling in near-real-time. *NASA Johnson Space Center Seventh Annual Workshop on Space Operations Applications and Research (SOAR 1993), 1*: 313-320.

Liang, T., Cannon, D.M., & Leifer, L.J. (1998). Augmenting the effectiveness of a design capture and reuse system based on direct observations of usage. *Proceedings of the International Conference on Design Theory and Methodology.*

Milne, A., & Leifer, L. (1999). The ecology of innovation in engineering design. Paper presented at the International Conference on Engineering Design (ICED'99), Munich, Germany.

Minneman, S. (1991). *The social construction of a technical reality: empirical studies of group engineering design practice.* (Unpublished doctoral dissertation). Stanford University, Stanford, CA.

Rill, B.R., & Hämäläinen, M.M. (2018). *The Art of Co-Creation: A Guidebook for Practitioners* (pp. 220). Singapore: Palgrave Macmillan.

Shedletsky, A., Campbell, M., & Havskjold, D. (2009). Embracing ambiguity: A perspective on student foresight engineering. *DS 58-10: Proceedings of ICED 09, the 17th International Conference on Engineering Design, 10*: 237-244.

Skogstad, P.L.S. (2009). *A unified innovation process model for engineering designers and managers* (Unpublished doctoral dissertation). Stanford University, Stanford, CA.

von Unold, B. (2017). *Fostering innovations by contextual empathic design* (Unpublished doctoral dissertation). Stanford University, Stanford, CA. Available at https://purl.stanford.edu/bz632cy8977

Wiesche, M., Leifer, L., Uebernickel, F., Lang, M., Byler, E., Feldmann, N., Garcia-Cifuentes, J.P., Höltää-Otto, K., Kelly, K., Satzger, G., Suzuki, S., Thong, C., Vignoli, M., & Krcmar, H. (2018). Teaching innovation in interdisciplinary environments: toward a design thinking syllabus. *Proceedings of the AIS SIGED 2018 (International Conference on Information Systems Education and Research).*

Team Performance & Assessment

Cockayne, W., Feland III, J.M., & Leifer, L. (2003). Using the contextual skills matrix for PBL assessment. *International Journal of Engineering Education, 19*(5): 701-705.

Feland III, J.M., & Leifer, L.J. (2001). Requirement volatility metrics as an assessment instrument for design team performance prediction. *International Journal of Engineering Education, 17*(4-5): 489-492.

Isaacs, E., & Tang, J.C. (1994). What video can and cannot do for collaboration: a case study. *Multimedia Systems, 2*(2): 63-73.

Leifer, L.J., & Steinert, M. (2014). Dancing with ambiguity: Causality behavior, design thinking, and triple-loop-learning. In: Gassmann O., Schweitzer F. (Eds.), *Management of the*

Fuzzy Front End of Innovation. Berlin, Germany: Springer.

Leifer L. (1998) Design-team performance: Metrics and the impact of technology. In: S.M. Brown & C.J. Seidner (Eds.), *Evaluating Corporate Training: Models and Issues, 46*: 297-319.

Leifer, L., & Toye, G. (1998). Instrumenting the collaborative-learning environment from pragmatic results to philosophical foundations.

Mabogunje, A., Leifer, L.J., Levitt, R.E., & Baudin, C. (1995). ME210-VDT: A managerial framework for measuring and improving design process performance. *Proceedings of Frontiers in Education 1995 25th Annual Conference. Engineering Education for the 21st Century, 1*: 3a5.20-3a5.26.

Mabogunje, A. & Leifer, L.J. (1996). 210-NP: measuring the mechanical engineering design process. *Technology-Based Re-Engineering Engineering Education Proceedings of Frontiers in Education FIE'96 26th Annual Conference, 3*: 1322-1328.

Mabogunje, A. (2003). Towards a conceptual framework for predicting engineering design team performance based on question asking activity simulation. In U. Lindemann (Ed.), *Human Behaviour in Design* (pp. 154-163). Berlin, Germany: Springer.

Tang, J., & Leifer, L. (1988). A framework for understanding the workspace activity of design teams. *Proceedings of the 1988 ACM conference on Computer-Supported Cooperative Work*: 244-249.

Tang, J.C., & Leifer, L.J. (1991). An observational methodology for studying group design activity. *Research in Engineering Design, 2*(4): 209-219

Stenholm, D., Moore, D., Leifer, L., & Bergsjö, D. (2018). Fail early, fail often: Exploring Stanford's ME310 course as a basis to improve innovation outpost efficacy. *DS 92: Proceedings of the DESIGN 2018 15th International Design Conference*: 2505-2516.

Wodehouse, A., Breslin, C., Eris, O., Grierson, H., Ion, W., Jung, M., Leifer, L., Mabogunje, A., & Sonalkar, N. (2007). A reflective approach to learning in a global design project. *Proceedings of the 9th International Conference on Engineering and Product Design Education.*

Teamwork & Collaboration

Brereton, M., Cannon, D.M., Mabogunje, A., & Leifer, L.J. (1994). *Characteristics of Collaboration in Engineering Design Teams: Mediating Design Progress through Social Interaction.*

Kress, G. & Sadler, J. (2014). Team cognition and reframing behavior: The impact of team cognition on problem reframing, team dynamics and design performance. In: L. Leifer, H. Plattner, & C. Meinel (Eds), *Design Thinking Research: Building Innovation Eco-Systems* (pp. 35-48). Berlin, Germany: Springer.

Kress, G.L., & Schar, M. (2012). Teamology – the art and science of design team formation. In: H. Plattner, C. Meinel, & L. Leifer (Eds.), *Design Thinking Research: Measuring Performance in Context* (pp. 189-209). Berlin, Germany: Springer.

Lande, M.J. (2012). *Designing and engineering: Ambidextrous mindsets for innovation* (Unpublished doctoral dissertation). Stanford University, Stanford, CA. Available at http://purl.stanford.edu/wz932pk5954

Larsson, A. (2003). Making sense of collaboration: the challenge of thinking together in global design teams. *Proceedings of the 2003 international ACM SIGGROUP conference on Supporting Group Work*: 153-160.

Reddy, J.M., Chan, B., & Finger, S. (1996). Patterns in design discourse: A case study. In: T. Tomiyama., M. Mäntylä, & S. Finger(Eds.), *Knowledge Intensive CAD (Volume 1*, pp. 265-283). Berlin, Germany: Springer.

Schar, M., & Lande, M. (2012). "What counts factors": Preparing engineering students to innovate through leadership of multi-functional teams. Paper presented at 2012 ASEE Annual Conference & Exposition, San Antonio, Texas.

Wilde, D. J. (1997). Using student preferences to guide design team composition. *Proceedings of DETC '97 1997 ASME Design Engineering Technical Conferences.*

Wilde, D. J. (2009). *Teamology: The Construction and Organization of Effective Teams.* London: Springer.

Team Coaching

Geva, U., & van der Loos, M. (2015). Coaching for design thinking. Available at https://hci.stanford.edu/dschool/resources/coaching/CoachingForDesignThinking.pdf

Grierson, H., Ion, W., & Juster, N. (2006). Project memories: Documentation and much more for global team design. *Proceedings of the 8th International Conference on Engineering and Product Design Education.*

Grimheden, M., van der Loos, M., Chen, H.L., Cannon, D.M., & Leifer, L.J. (2006). Culture coaching: A model for facilitating globally distributed collaborative work. *Proceedings from Frontiers in Education 36th Annual Conference.*

Häger, F., Kowark, T., & Uflacker, M. (2016). Experience and knowledge transfer through special topic coaching sessions. In: H. Plattner, C. Meinel, & L. Leifer (Eds)., *Design Thinking Research* (pp 187-201). Berlin, Germany: Springer.

Reich, Y., Ullmann, G., Van der Loos, M. & Leifer, L. (2009). Coaching product development teams: a conceptual foundation for empirical studies. *Research in Engineering Design, 19*(4): 205-222.

Design Tools & Prototyping

Analytis, S., Sadler, J.A., Cutkosky, M.R. (2017). Creating paper robots increases designers' confidence to prototype with microcontrollers and electronics. *International Journal of Design Creativity and Innovation, 5*(1-2): 48-59.

Berglund, A., & Leifer, L. (2012). For whom are we prototyping? A review of the role of conceptual prototyping in engineering design creativity. *DS 73-2 Proceedings of the 2nd International conference on Design Creativity, 2*: 201-210.

Brereton, M. (1998). *The role of hardware in learning engineering fundamentals: an empirical study of engineering design and product analysis activity* (Unpublished doctoral dissertation). Stanford University, Stanford, CA.

Bushnell, T., Steber, S., Matta, A., Cutkosky, M., & Leifer, L. (2013). Using a 'Dark Horse' prototype to manage innovative teams. *Proceedings of the 3rd International Conference of Integration of Design, Engineering & Management for Innovation.*

Design Factory Melbourne. (2016, October 20). Key learnings

about innovation through a playful Paper Bike Race [Web log post]. Available at https://medium.com/@DFMelbourne

Durão, L.F.C.S., Kelly, K., Nakano, D.N., Zancul, E., & McGinn, C.L. (2018). Divergent prototyping effect on the final design solution: the role of "Dark Horse" prototype in innovation projects. *Procedia CIRP, 70*: 265-271.

Hong, J., Toye, G., & Leifer, L. (1994). Using the WWW for a team-based engineering design class. *Proceedings of the 2nd WWW Conference,* Chicago, Illinois.

Hong, J., & Leifer, L. (1995). Using the WWW to support project-team formation. *Proceedings From Frontiers in Education 1995 25th Annual Conference. Engineering Education for the 21st Century.*

Hong, J., Toye, G., & Leifer, L.J. (1996). Engineering design notebook for sharing and reuse. *Computers in Industry, 29*(1–2): 27-35.

Hutterer, P., Eris ,O., Jung, M., Leifer, L., Lindemann, U., & Mabogunje, A. (2004). What do designers really need? An explorative experiment before developing teaching tools and methods. Paper presented at IADIS International Conference Cognition and Exploratory Learning in Digital Age (CELDA 2004), Lisbon, Portugal.

Jablokow, K., & Spreckelmeyer, K. (2014). Exploring the impact of cognitive style and academic discipline on design prototype variability. Paper presented at the ASEE 2014 Annual Conference, Indianapolis, Indiana.

Toye, G., Cutkosky, M., Leifer, L., Tenebaum, M., & Glicksman, J. (1994). SHARE: A methodology and environment for collaborative product development. *International Journal of Cooperative Information Systems, 3*(2): 129-153.

Global Adaptation

Camacho, M. (2015). Design thinking in development: an emerging story. Transferring design thinking knowledge from Stanford University to the Colombian context. In *Emerging Practices: Inquiry into the Developing.* Shanghai, China: Tongji University Press.

Cannon, D.M., & Leifer, L.J. (2001). ME110K: An exploratory course in cross-cultural, project-based design education. *International Journal of Engineering Education, 17*(4&5): 410-415.

Fukuzaki, A., & Fukuda, S. (1999). Convergent knowledge generation development of concept and framework for distance learning. *Proceedings from 1999 IEEE International Conference on Systems, Man, and Cybernetics, 2*: 220-224.

Fukuda, S., Kostov, V., & Fukuzaki, A. (1999). What we have learned from our experience from TMIT-Stanford shared class. *IEEE SMC'99 Conference Proceedings, 2*: 230-234.

García-Cifuentes, J.P. (2016). Design thinking para innovar, desde la interdisciplinariedad e interculturalidad, en ingeniería. Paper presented at Encuentro Internacional de Educación en Ingeniería ACOFI 2016, Cartagena, Colombia.

Hillen, V., & Levy, P. (2013). People, place, process: Lessons learnt the way of a d.school. Paper presented at the International Conference on Engineering Design (ICED) 2013, Seoul, Korea.

Hillen, V. (2015). 101 *Repères Pour Innover.* Self published.

Hillen, V. (2016). The Paris d.school. In: B. Banerjee & S. Ceri (Eds.), *Creating Innovation Leaders: A Global Perspective* (pp. 227-237). Berlin, Germany: Springer.

Kowark, T., Häger, F., Gehrer, R., & Krüger, J. (2014). A research plan for the integration of design thinking with large scale software development projects. In: L. Leifer, H. Plattner, & C. Meinel (Eds.), *Design Thinking Research: Building Innovation Eco-Systems* (pp 183-202). Berlin, Germany: Springer.

Skogstad, P.L., Currano, R.M., & Leifer, L.J. (2008). An experiment in design pedagogy transfer across cultures and disciplines. *International Journal of Engineering Education, 24*: 367-376.

Suzuki, S., & Leifer, L. (2009). Student Facebook connections in a global project based engineering design course. *DS 58-10: Proceedings of ICED 09, the 17th International Conference on Engineering Design, 10*: 215-226.

Uebernickel, F., Brenner, W., Naef, T., Pukall, B. & Schindlholzer, B. (2015). *Design Thinking: Das Handbuch*. Frankfurt, Germany: Frankfurter Allgemeine Buch.

Personal Experience

Lumiaho, M. (2014, November 11). Educational impact: ME310 global design innovation course [Web log post]. Available at http://medium.com/@mlumiaho

Moreira, J. (2018, January 18). How the perspective of looking to the world and myself changed [Web log post]. Available at https://medium.com/@joanamoreirapt

Oliveira, A. (2017, July 26). The future global innovation leaders – ME310 Stanford – my journey [Web log post]. Available at https://medium.com/@oliveira

Network Maps

Before the mid-2000s, Stanford ME310 faculty occasionally hosted visiting professors and foreign scholars to the class. From 2005 on, ME310 began to formally partner with a growing network of global academic institutions on student projects, which has helped spawn the pedagogy more broadly across the world. In turn, these partners have adapted the ME310 approach for their university course (or lab) and with other regional partners. In particular, Aalto University's teaching team has carried the annual tradition of creating intertwined ME310-global and SUGAR Network maps since 2008. Incidentally, some schools have partnered on multiple projects in an academic year. Note the data tables here are incomplete, as they stop at AY2018. — *Editor*

ME310–Global Network Map
AY2005

ME310–Global Network Map
AY2006

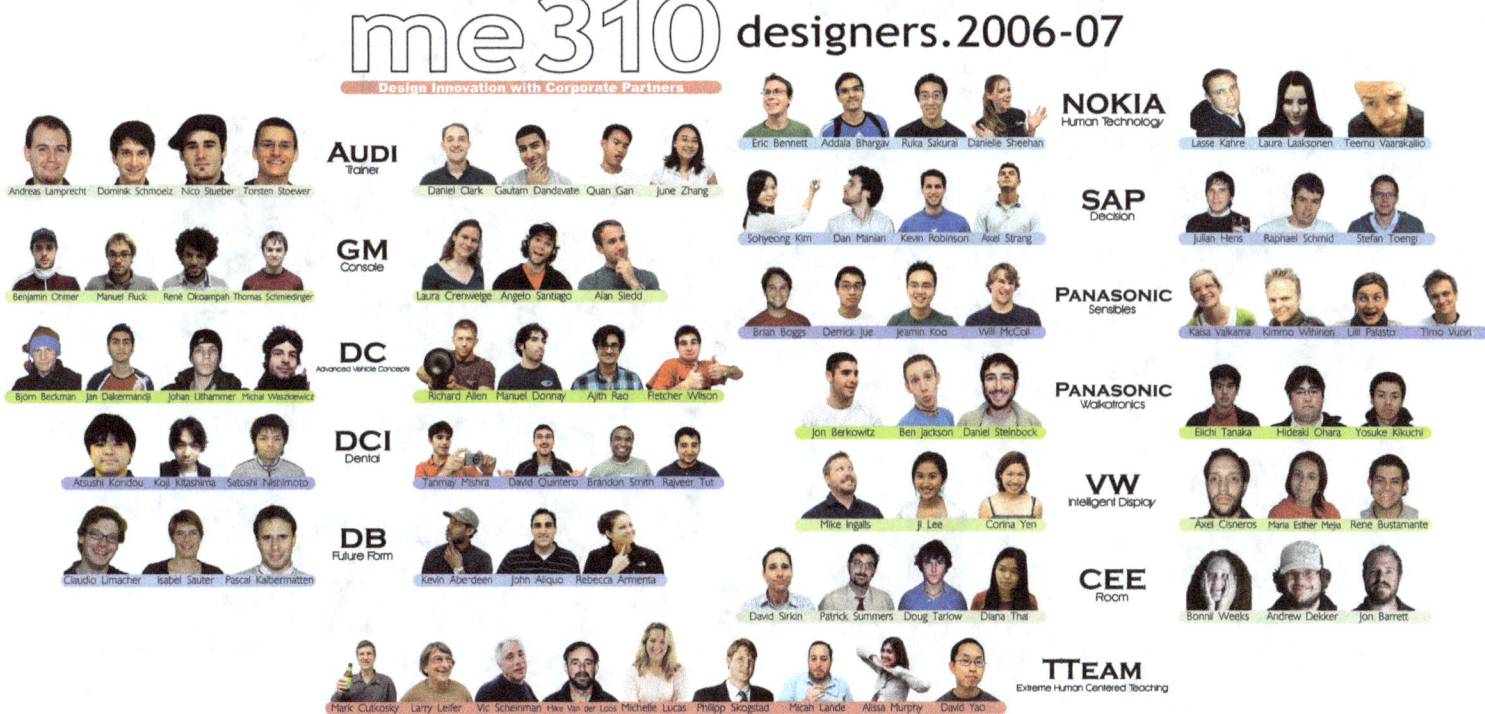

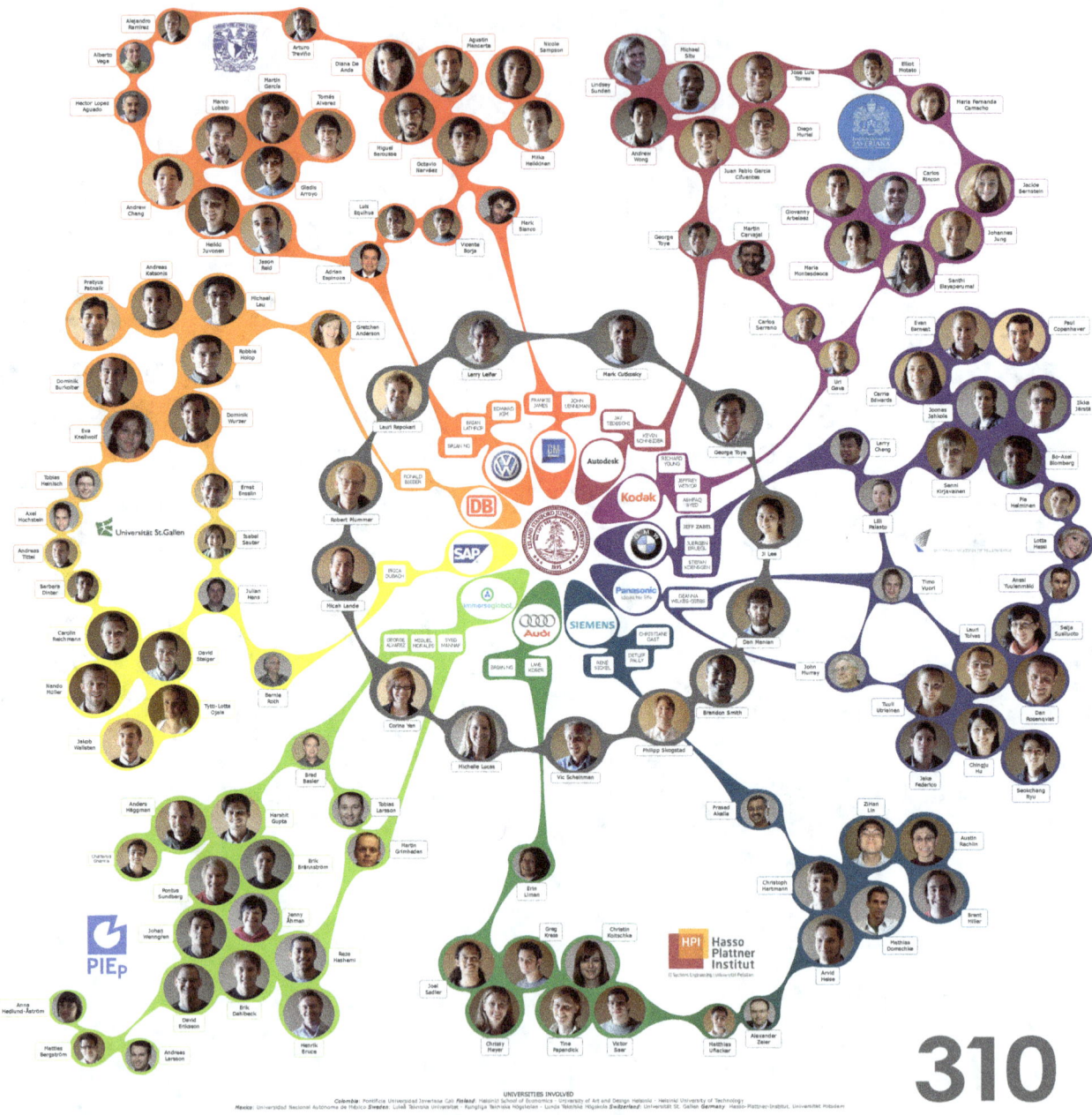

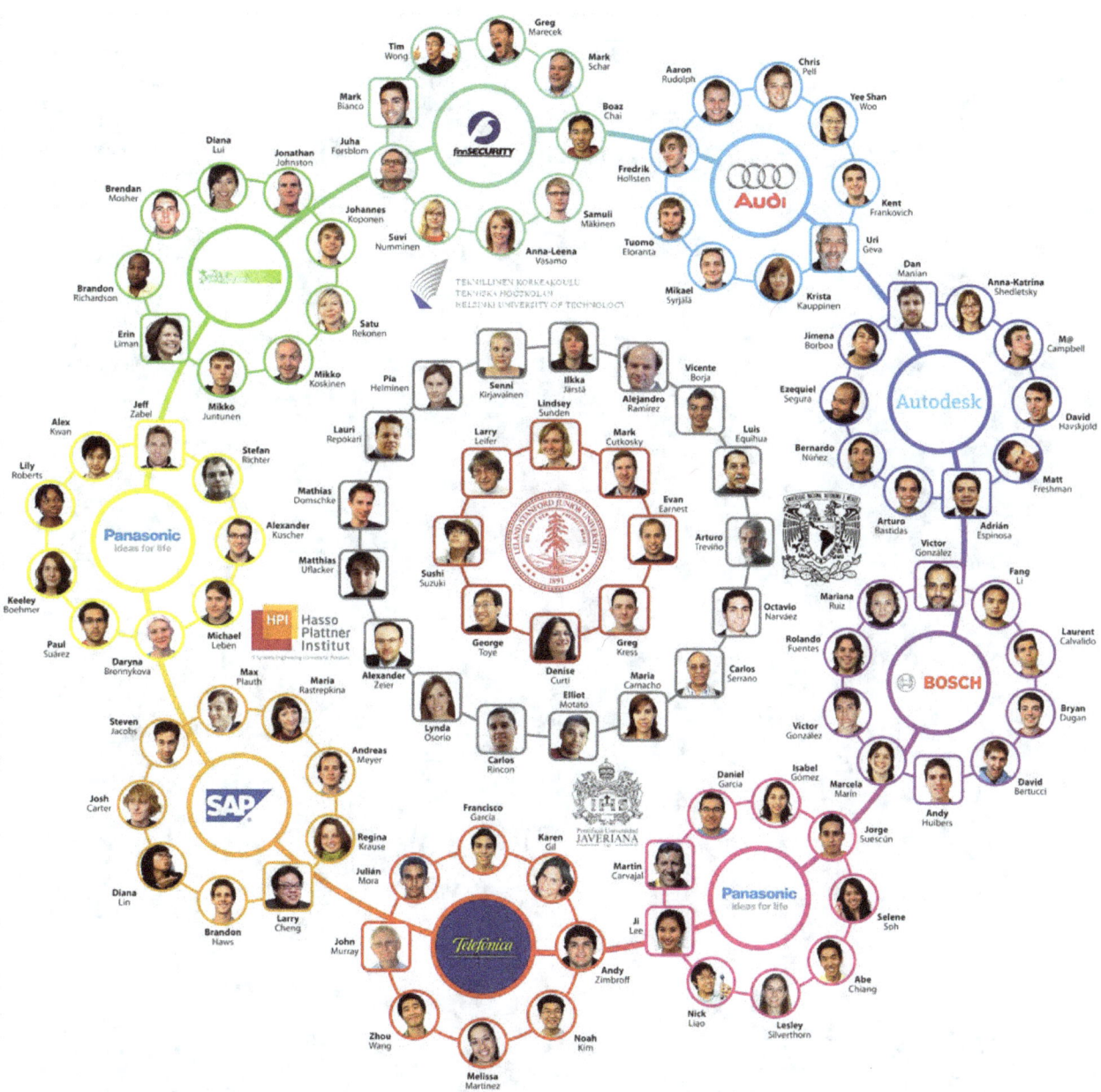

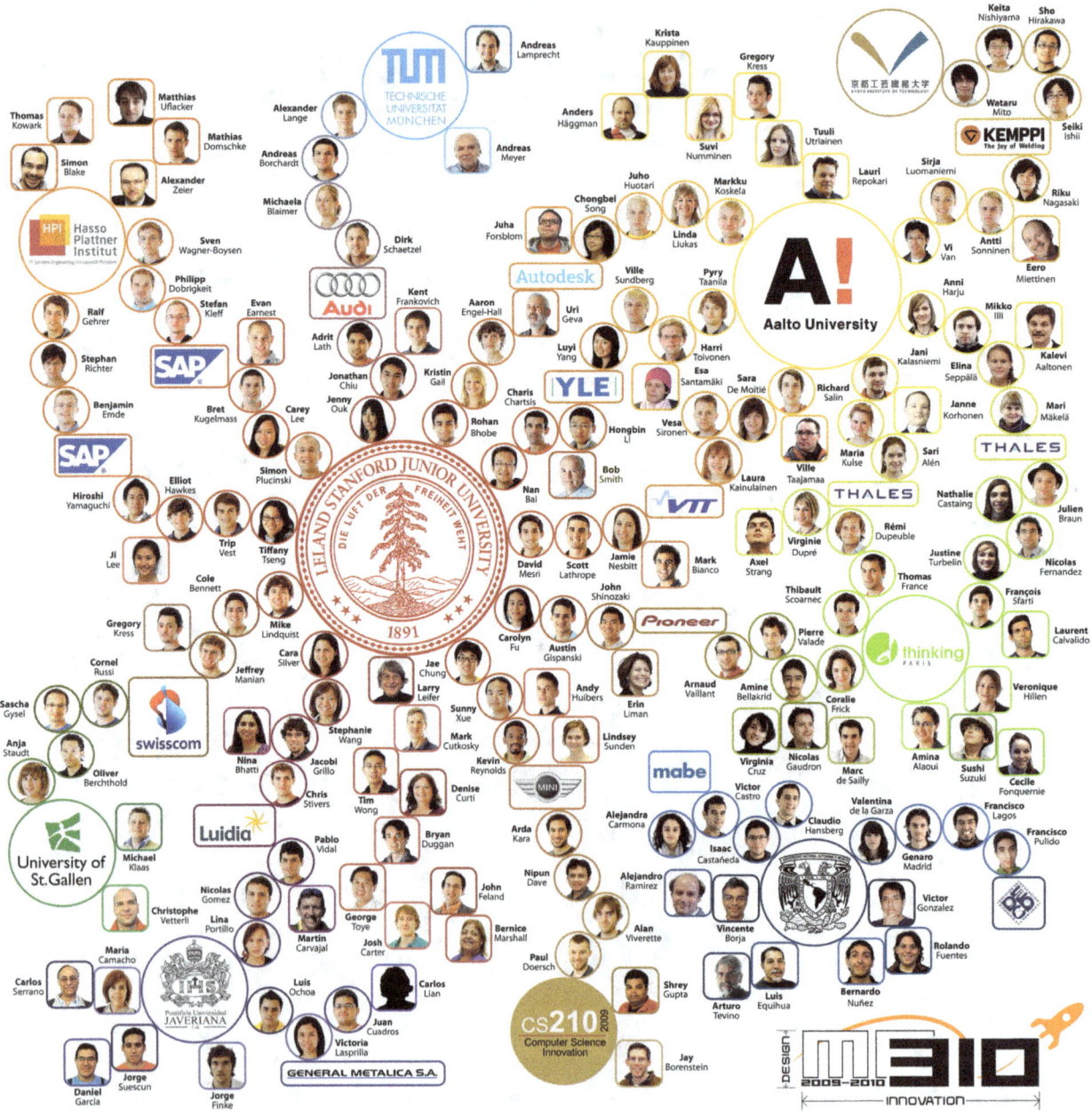

ME310–Global and SUGAR Network Map
AY2010

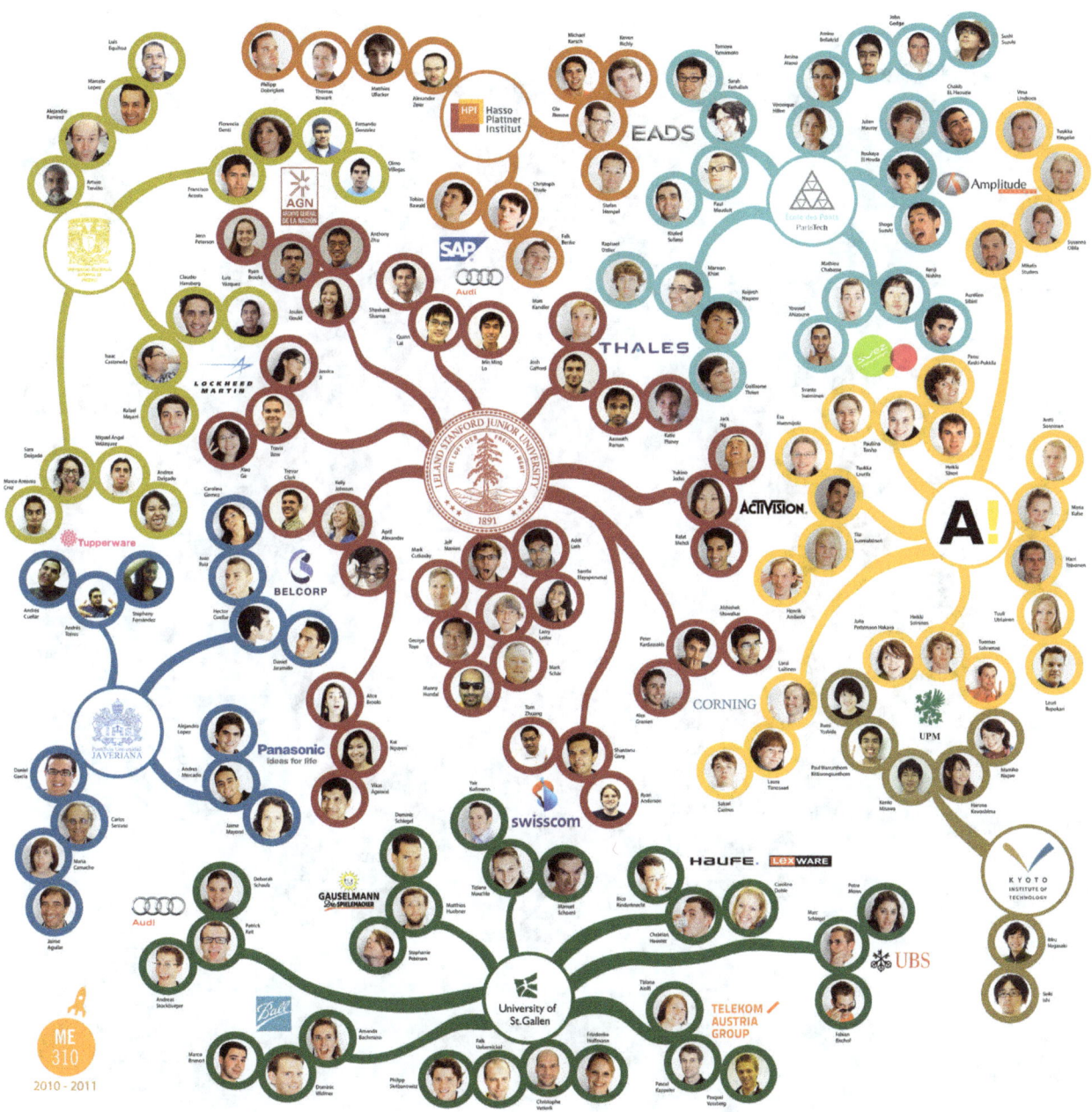

ME310–Global Network Map
AY2011

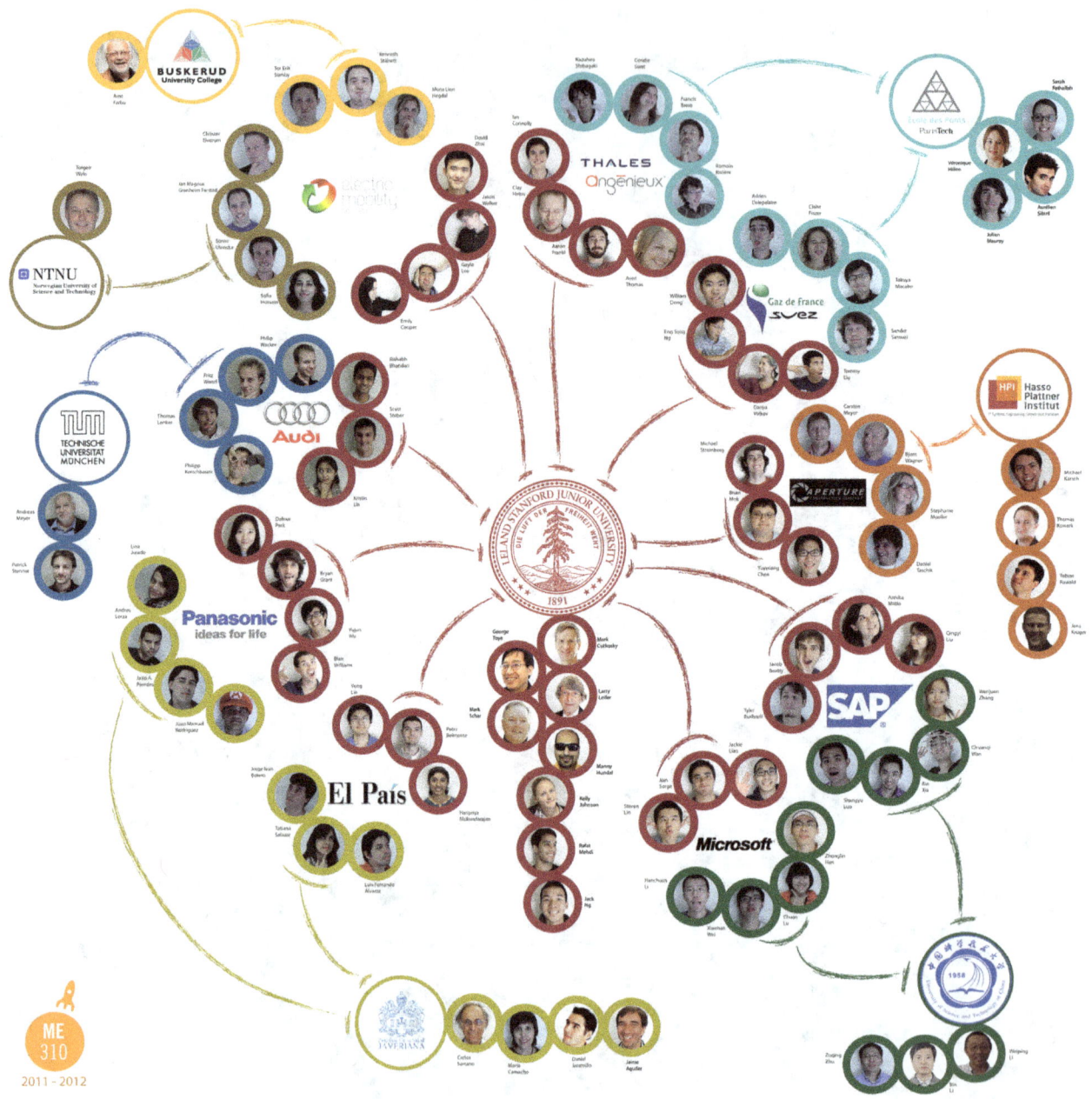

ME310 at Stanford University 50 Years of Redesign (1967–2017)

ME310–Global and SUGAR Network Map
AY2012

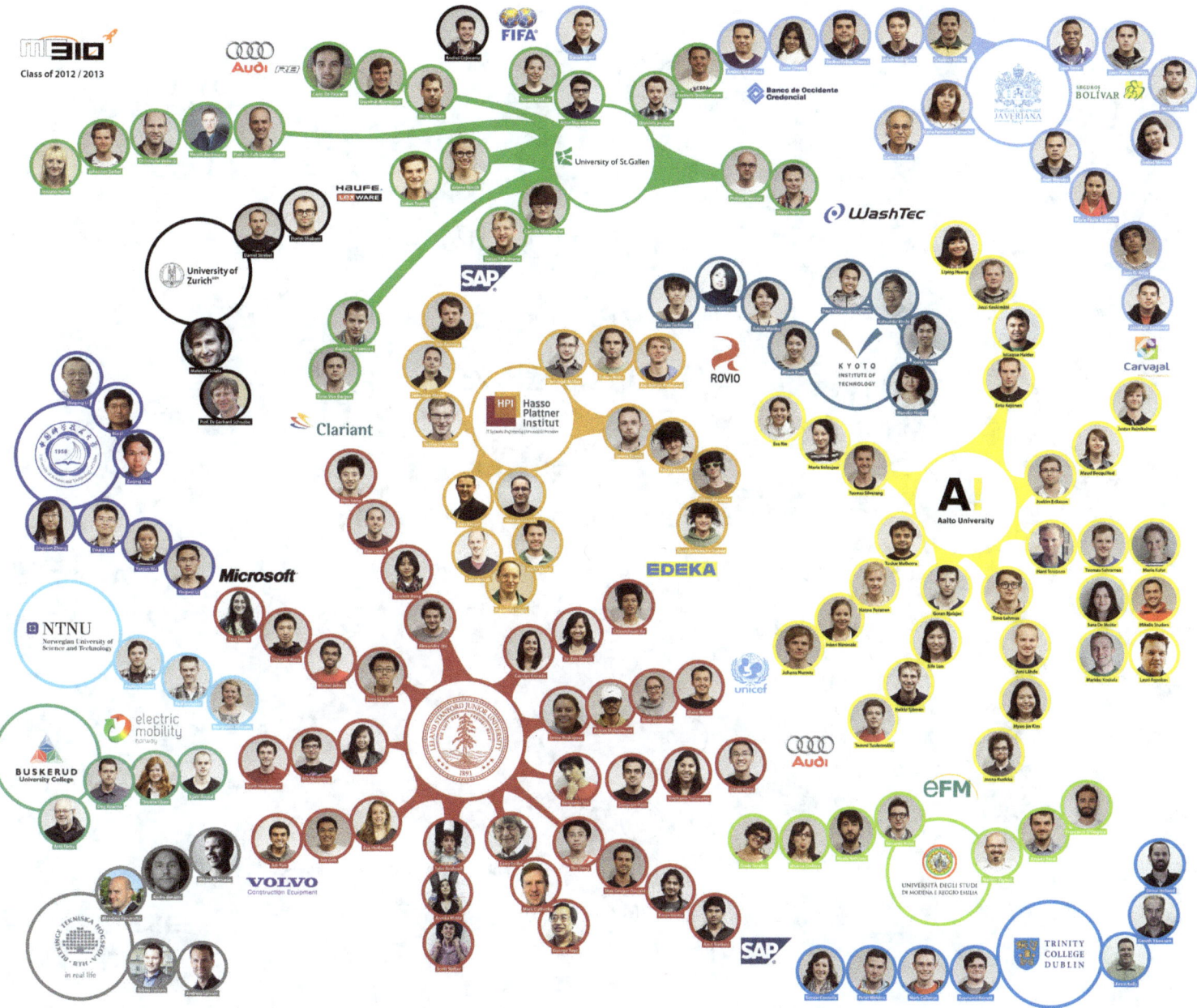

ME310–Global and SUGAR Network Map
AY2013

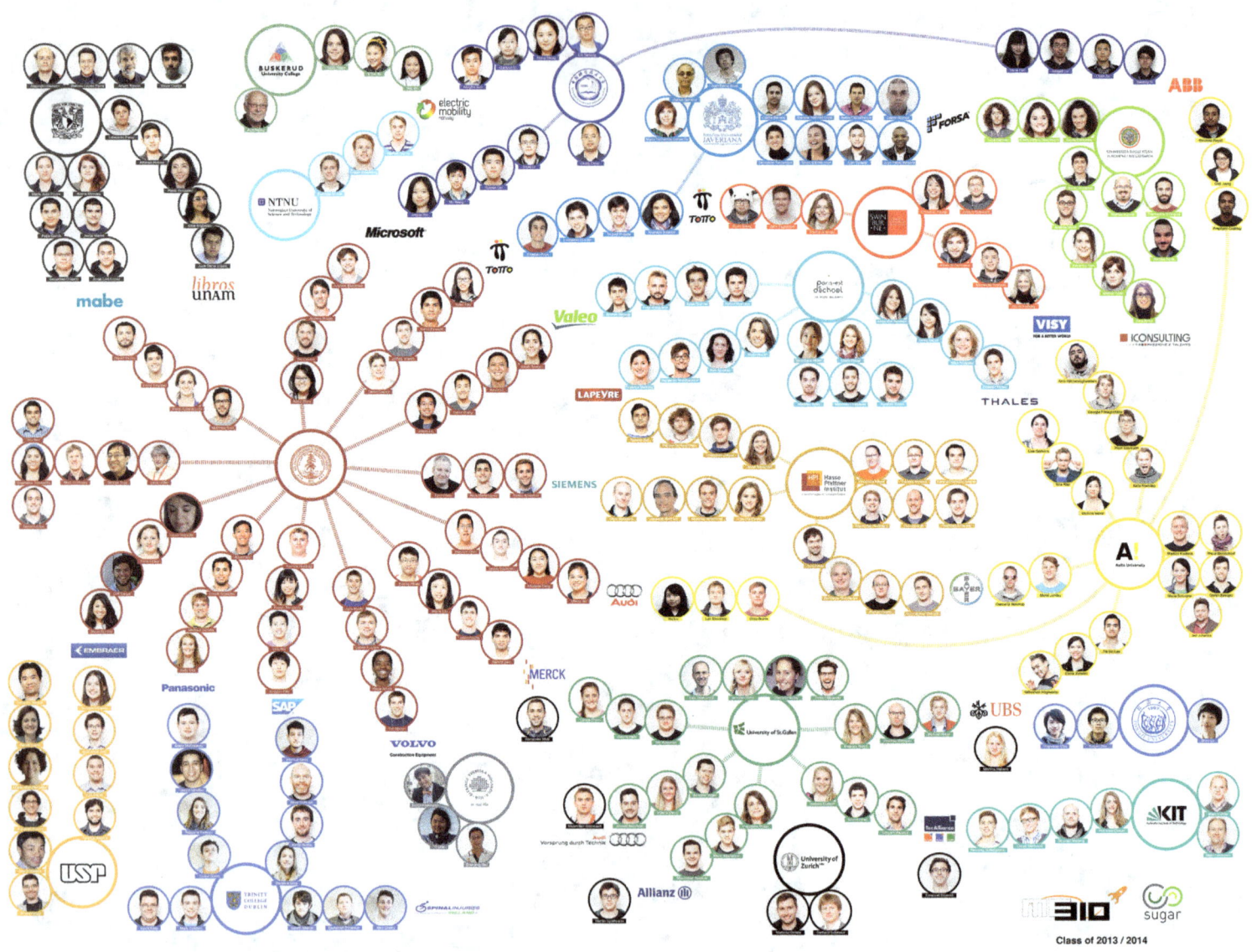

Class of 2013 / 2014

ME310–Global and SUGAR Network Map
AY2014

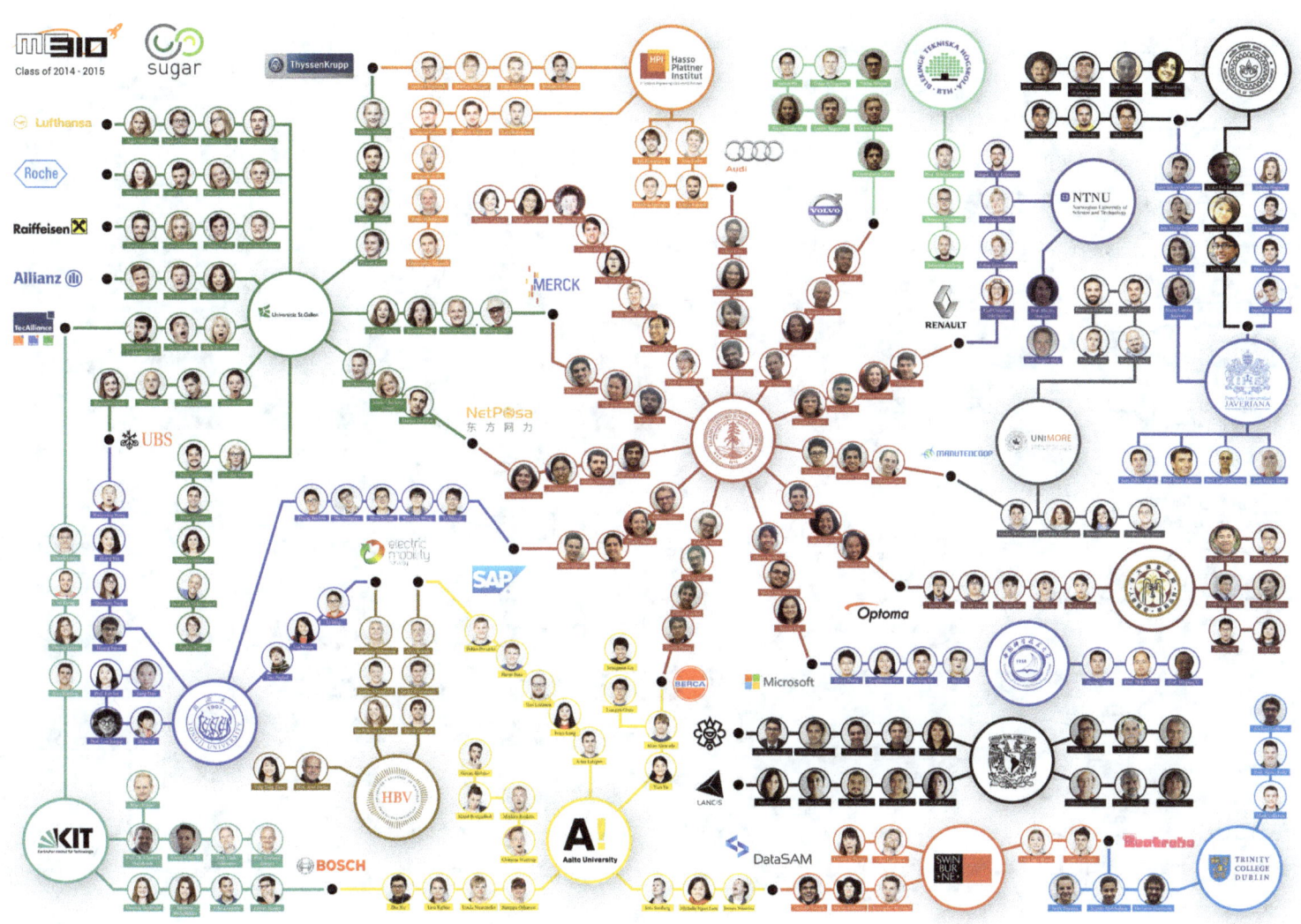

ME310–Global and SUGAR Network Map
AY2015

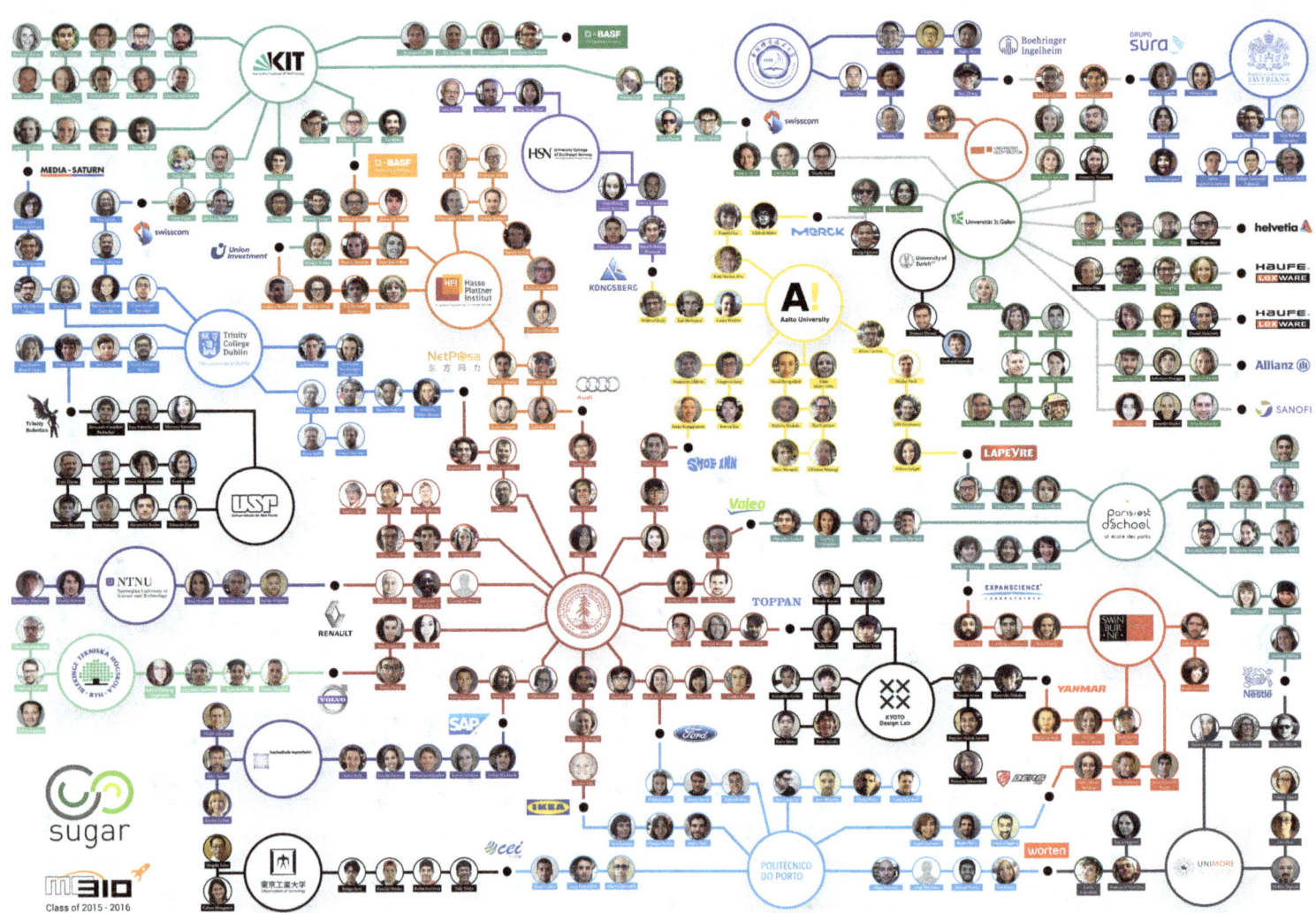

ME310–Global and SUGAR Network Map
AY2016

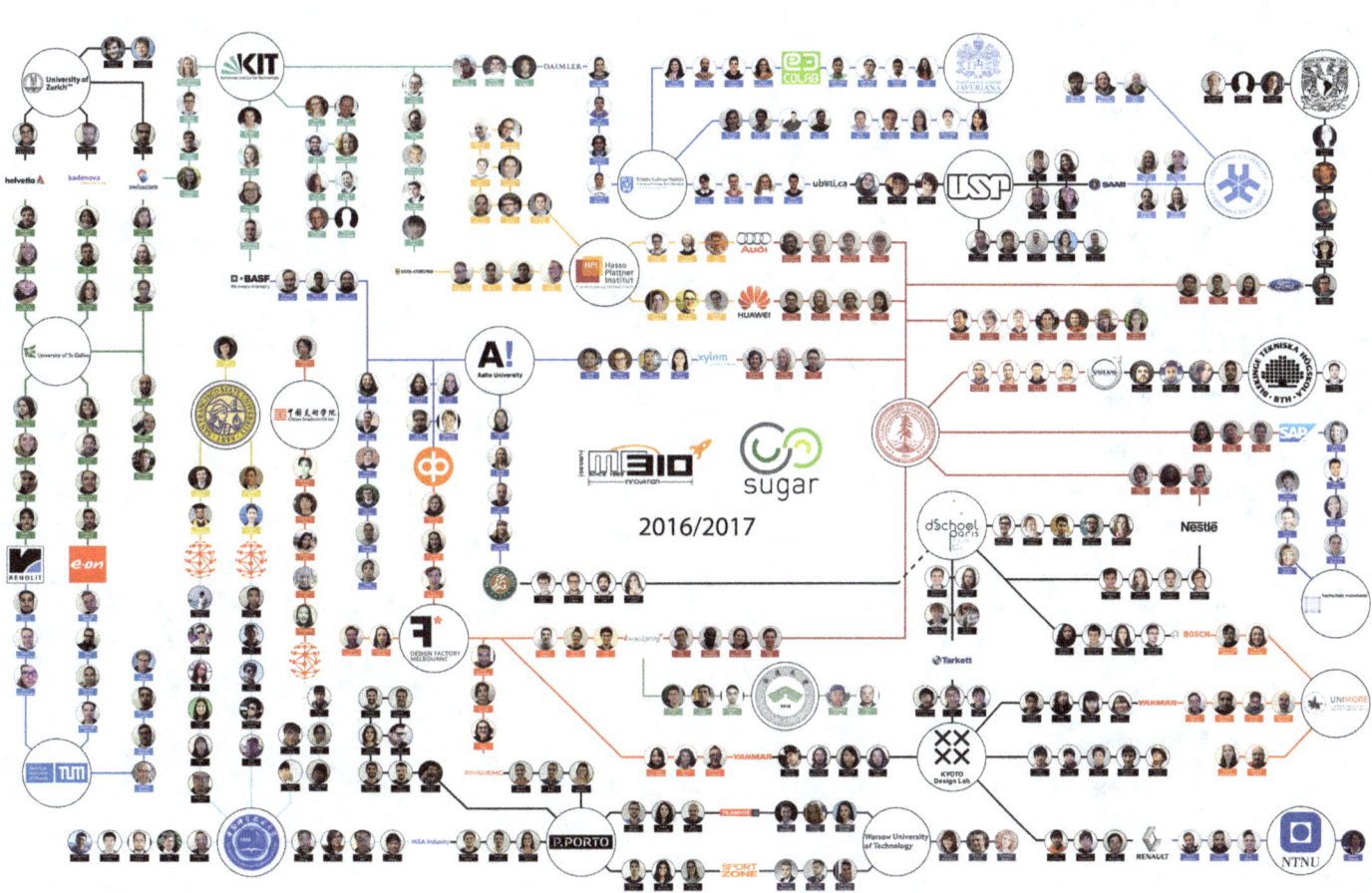

ME310 Academic Partners — Europe

SCHOOL	COUNTRY	AY2006	AY2007	AY2008	AY2009	AY2010	AY2011	AY2012	AY2013	AY2014	AY2015	AY2016	AY2017
Aalto University (includes Helsinki University of Technology – TKK)	Finland	•	•	•	•	•		•	•	•	•	•	•
Blekinge Institute of Technology (BTH)	Sweden								•	•	•	•	•
École des Ponts ParisTech / d.school Paris	France				•	•	•		•		•	•	•
Hasso Plattner Institute (HPI)	Germany		•		•	•	•	•	•	•	•	•	•
Linköping University	Sweden												•
Norwegian University of Science and Technology (NTNU)	Norway						•	•		•	•		
Polytechnic Institute of Porto	Portugal										•	•	
Royal Institute of Technology (KTH)	Sweden	•	•										
Technical University of Munich (TUM)	Germany	•			•		•						
Trinity College	Ireland							•	•		•		
University College of Southeast Norway (includes Buskerud University College)	Norway						•	•		•			
University of Mannheim	Germany										•	•	•
University of Modena and Reggio Emilia (UNIMORE)	Italy									•			
University of St. Gallen (HSG)	Switzerland	•	•		•			•	•	•			

ME310 Academic Partners — Asia

SCHOOL	COUNTRY	AY2006	AY2007	AY2008	AY2009	AY2010	AY2011	AY2012	AY2013	AY2014	AY2015	AY2016	AY2017
Beijing Normal University	China												●
Fukuoka Institute of Technology	Japan	●											
Kyoto Institute of Technology	Japan				●						●		
Nantong University	China											●	
National Taiwan University	Taiwan									●			
Tongji University	China									●			
University of Science and Technology of China	China						●	●	●	●			
University of Tokyo	Japan	●											

ME310 Academic Partners — Australia

SCHOOL	COUNTRY	AY2006	AY2007	AY2008	AY2009	AY2010	AY2011	AY2012	AY2013	AY2014	AY2015	AY2016	AY2017
Swinburne University	Australia								•			•	•
University of Queensland	Australia	•											

ME310 Academic Partners — Latin America

SCHOOL	COUNTRY	AY2006	AY2007	AY2008	AY2009	AY2010	AY2011	AY2012	AY2013	AY2014	AY2015	AY2016	AY2017
Pontificia Universidad Javeriana	Colombia		•		•	•	•		•				
University of São Paulo	Brazil								•				
Universidad Nacional Autónoma de México	Mexico	•	•			•			•			•	

Contributors

Contributors
In alphabetical order

Adams, Jesse
117

Adams, James 'Jim'
v, **4**, 8, 11, 15, **26**, 40, **54**, 90, 92, 93, 94, 154, 201

Aldaz, Gabriel
118, 119

Analytis, Santhi (Elayaperumal)
131, 171

Anderson, Gary
90

Asseily, Alex
118, 119

Baya, Vinod
107, 168, 169

Bernhelm, Jackie (Bernstein)
132

Bianco, Mark
130

Bitar, Sami
115

Bonnstetter, Darren
110

Bushnell, Tyler
144, 171

Byler, Eric
100, 169

Carleton, Tamara
v, 168

Cagan, Laird
96

Camacho, Maria
73, 74, **75**, 76, 168, 172

Cannon, David
50, **102**, 105, 169, 170, 171, 172

Carter, Josh
138

Cooper, Tom
96

Currano, Becky
125, 173

Cutkosky, Mark
11, **18**, 22, 29, **39**, 41, **44**, 50, **55**, 62, 70, 105, 119, 127, 130, 133, 134, 136, 137, 141, 161, 171, 172, 201

Duggan, Bryan
139

Ecklund, Kreig
114

Elfsberg, Jenny
35

Fuchs, Henry
v, 5, **8**, **9**, 26, 93, 154

Flatté, Anne
120, 168

Häggman, Anders
134, **136**, 201

Heikkinen, Mikka
134, 136

Hight, Tim
94

Jais, Alexandre
144

Junqua, Jean-Claude
28

Kelley, David
95, 168

Khan, Rafay
112

Lande, Micah
55, **130**, 170, 171

Larsson, Tobias
83

Leifer, Larry
vi, 11, 12, **15**, 20, 22, 28, 29, 31, **38**, 40, 41, 44, **49**, 50, **62**, 69, **70**, 71, 72, 73, 74, 75, 76, 78, 101, 104, 105, 110, 112, 114, 115, 117, 118, 119, 122, 127, 128, 130, 133, 134, 136, 137, 138, 141, 144, 157, 158, 159, 160, 161, 168, 169, 170, 171, 172, 173, 201

Lin, Yong
145, **147**

Litherland, Craig
118, **119**

Lotz, Jeff
96

Mabogunje, Ade
104, 114, 168, 170, 172

Manian, Dan
131

Martin Rygiert, Yvonne
84

Matsui, Kenji
31, **51**

McNelly, Michael 'Mike'
41

Næss, Leif
81

Neeley, Lawrence
121, 169

Pell, Chris
140

Piziali, Robert 'Bob'
9, 93, 95, 96, 155

Radcliffe, David
11, **12**, **49**, 105, 114

Richardson, Brandon
138

Roth, Bernard 'Bernie'
11, 12, 40, 44, 49, **54**, 90, 93, 94, 105, 114

Salazar, Tatiana
145

Schar, Mark
141, 170, 171

Schindlholzer, Bernhard
71, 77, 173

Seering, Warren
92, 137

Serrano, Carlos
76

Skogstad, Philipp
71, 74, 75, 77, **126**, 128, 169, 173

Sonalkar, Neeraj
105, **127**, 170

Steinbeck, Reinhold
20, **73**, 75, 168

Sunden, Lindsey
133

Suzuki, Sushi
128, 169, 173

Tombelli, Teresa
148

Toye, George
20, **22**, 130, 141, 169, 170, 172, 201

Uebernickel, Falk
71, 77, **78**, 169, 173

Vetterli, Christophe
77

Vignoli, Matteo
80, 169

Wilde, Doug
39, **40**, 41, 93, 94, 171

Wilkes-Gibbs, Deanna
29

Wong, Tim
142

Yang, Maria
116, 137

Yen, Sam
117

Image Sources

Image Sources

We are grateful to numerous people who shared their personal photo collections with us. We owe a special thanks to Stanford Libraries and Stanford Daily newspaper for printing permission rights. Images are listed below by page number and page location. Where multiple images are presented on a page, please refer to the legend as follows for the corresponding image location. An asterisk has been used to denote if additional editing or modifications (beyond simple perspective-, color-, or cropping adjustments) were made to an image.

Legend:
H – Headshot
T – Top
M – Middle (y-axis)
B – Bottom
L – Left
C – Center (x-axis)
R – Right
BG – Background

At times, we intentionally include lower resolution photos to help tell the ME310 story when higher resolution photos were unavailable.

Front Matter
iii	Warren Seering
iv	Anders Häggman
v–H	Tamara Carleton
v–BG	Tamara Carleton
vi	Tamara Carleton
vii	Stanford University; Instagram.com post on June 27, 2018

Learning
002	Anders Häggman
004–H	James Adams
004–BG	James L. Adams Papers (SC0949), Department of Special Collections & University Archives, Stanford Libraries
006*	James L. Adams Papers (SC0949), Department of Special Collections & University Archives, Stanford Libraries *[enhanced using resources provided by lstore.graphics]*
007*	Warren Seering *[enhanced using resources provided by Antoniu at fuzzimo.com]*
008–H	James L. Adams Papers (SC0949), Department of Special Collections & University Archives, Stanford Libraries
008–BG	ibid.
009	https://www.exponent.com/professionals/p/piziali-robert-l
010*	James L. Adams Papers (SC0949). Department of Special Collections & University Archives, Stanford Libraries. *[enhanced using resources provided by lstore.graphics]*
011–H	https://www.researchgate.net/figure/Professor-Roth-circa-20-0-0_fig2_321466099
011–BG	Miika Heikkinen
012–H	LinkedIn.com, David Radcliffe personal page
012–BG	David Radcliffe
013–T	Sushi Suzuki
013–B	Sushi Suzuki
014*	Philipp Skogstad, presentation slides for Volkswagen AutoUni: ME310 Collaboration *[enhanced using resources provided by Antoniu at fuzzimo.com]*
015–H	Larry Leifer
015–BG	Stanford Center for Professional Development, "ME210: An Experience in Product-Based Learning" video still, 1997
016	Stanford University, ME310 course archives
017	Stanford University, ME310 course archives
018–H	Mark Cutkosky

018–BG	Tyler Bushnell
019–L	Teresa Tombelli
019–R	Teresa Tombelli
020–H	Reinhold Steinbeck
020–BG	Reinhold Steinbeck
021–T	Reinhold Steinbeck
021–B	Reinhold Steinbeck
022–H	Stanford University Designing Education Lab faculty profile
022–BG	Stanford Center for Professional Development, "ME210: An Experience in Product-Based Learning" video still, 1997

Companies

024	Anders Häggman
026–H	James Adams
026–BG	James L. Adams Papers (SC0949). Department of Special Collections & University Archives, Stanford Libraries.
027	James L. Adams Papers (SC0949). Department of Special Collections & University Archives, Stanford Libraries.
028–H	LinkedIn.com, Jean-Claude Junqua personal page
028–BG	"Panawear" report, 2008, ME310 digital collection, Stanford Libraries, https://searchworks.stanford.edu/view/9528211
029–H	LinkedIn.com, Deanna Wilkes-Gibbs personal page
029–R*	Larry Leifer [enhanced using resources provided by lstore.graphics]
030*	Stanford University, ME310 course archives [enhanced using resources provided by lstore.graphics]
031–H	Kenji Matsui
031–BG	Kenji Matsui
032	"Aura" report, ME310 digital collection, Stanford Libraries, https://searchworks.stanford.edu/ view/ xy547ss8747
033*	Stanford Daily, volume 197, issue 39, 19 April 1990 [enhanced using resources provided by Hyperpix Studio at https://www.pixelsurplus.com/mockups/free-photorealistic-newspaper-mockup?ref=mockupworld]
034–L*	Stanford University, ME310 course archives [enhanced using resources provided by lstore.graphics]
034–R*	ibid.
035–H	Jenny Elfsberg
035–BG	Jenny Elfsberg
036	Jenny Elfsberg

Teams

038–H	Larry Leifer
038–BG	Stanford Center for Professional Development, "ME210: An Experience in Product-Based Learning" video still, 1997
039–H	Mark Cutkosky
093–B*	Mark Cutkosky, "Developments in (global) project-based design education" presentation slides, 2000
040–H	Stanford University School of Engineering faculty page
040–L	Excerpt reprinted by permission from Springer Customer Service Centre GmbH: Springer Nature, Teamology by Douglass J. Wilde, 2009
041	Amazon.com Michael McNelly author page
042*	Stanford Daily, volume 212, issue 26, 24 October 1997 [enhanced using resources provided by www.veila.com]
043	Mark Schar
044–H	Mark Cutkosky
044–R	Linda A. Cicero, Stanford News Service

045–L*   Stanford Daily, volume 206, issue 24, 26 October 1994 [enhanced using resources provided by www.veila.com]
045–R*   Stanford Daily, volume 210, issue 26, 25 October 1996 [enhanced using resources provided by www.veila.com]
046   Tamara Carleton
047   Mark Schar
048–L   Anders Häggman
048–R   Miika Heikkinen
049–T   Larry Leifer
049–B   LinkedIn.com, David Radcliffe personal page
050   LinkedIn.com, David Cannon personal page
051–H   Kenji Matsui
051–L*   Kenji Matsui [enhanced using resources provided by lstore.graphics]
051–R   Kenji Matsui
052*   ME310 loft poster, designer unknown [enhanced using resources provided by lstore.graphics]

Loft

054–T   James Adams
054–B   https://www.researchgate.net/figure/Professor-Roth-circa-20-0-0_fig2_321466099
055–T   Mark Cutkosky
055–L   Micah Lande
055–R*   Stanford Center for Professional Development, "ME210: An Experience in Product-Based Learning" video still, 1997 [enhanced using resources provided by Antoniu at fuzzimo.com]
056–L   Sushi Suzuki
056–C   Sushi Suzuki
056–R   Sushi Suzuki
057–L   Larry Leifer
057–R   Larry Leifer
058–059   Teresa Tombelli

Showcase

060   Sushi Suzuki
062–H   Larry Leifer
062–B   Facebook.com DesignEXPE group page
063*   Stanford Daily, volume 227, issue 59, 12 May 2005 [enhanced using resources provided by www.veila.com]
064–T   "A redesign of the San Francisco cable car grip" report, 1978, ME310 digital collection, Stanford Libraries, https://searchworks.stanford.edu/view/9527935
064–M   "Head control/smart wheelchair" report, 1980, ME310 digital collection, Stanford Libraries, https://searchworks.stanford.edu/view/9527944
064–B   "A speed controlled film handling device" report, 1983, ME310 digital collection, Stanford Libraries, https://searchworks.stanford.edu/view/9527971
065–T   "Single passenger commuter vehicle cockpit" report, 1991, ME310 digital collection, Stanford Libraries, https://searchworks.stanford.edu/view/9528054
065–M   "An intravenous flow control pump" report, 1986, ME310 digital collection, Stanford Libraries, https://searchworks.stanford.edu/view/9528000
065–B   "Ceramic breaking" report, 1990, ME310 digital collection, Stanford Libraries, https://searchworks.stanford.edu/view/9528044

066–T	"Single passenger commuter vehicle cockpit" report, 1991, ME310 digital collection, Stanford Libraries, https://searchworks.stanford.edu/view/9528054	067–B	"ME310 Team UNICEF final documentation" report, 2013, ME310 digital collection, Stanford Libraries, https://searchworks.stanford.edu/view/rh549nv9529	079	Tyler Bushnell
				080–H	LinkedIn.com Matteo Vignoli personal page
				080–BG	UNIMORE Design Thinking homepage
				081–H	LinkedIn.com Leif Næss personal page
066–M	"Dairy capping equipment" report, 1994, ME310 digital collection, Stanford Libraries, https://searchworks.stanford.edu/view/9528085			081–BG	Leif Næss
				082–L*	Leif Næss [enhanced using resources provided by lstore.graphics]

Global

068	Stanford Daily, volume 227, issue 59, 12 May 2005 [enhanced using resources provided by www.veila.com]
070–H	Larry Leifer
070–B	Facebook ME310 Aalto group page; January 12, 2017 post

082–R* Leif Næss [enhanced using resources provided by lstore.graphics]

066–B	"A faying surface area gap measurement apparatus for Boeing Commercial Airplane group" report, 1997, ME310 digital collection, Stanford Libraries, https://searchworks.stanford.edu/view/9528144	071–H	LinkedIn.com Bernhard Schindlholzer personal page	083–H	Tobias Larsson
				083–LM	Tobias Larsson
				083–LB	Tobias Larsson
		071–BG	TEDx Talks at FHKufstein; August 4, 2016; YouTube.com video still	083–CM	Tobias Larsson
				083–CB	Tobias Larsson
				083–R*	Tobias Larsson [enhanced using resources provided by lstore.graphics]
		072	Tamara Carleton		
067–T	"Artificial sense of direction for pedestrians (Sense-i)" report, 2007, ME310 digital collection, Stanford Libraries, https://searchworks.stanford.edu/view/9528195	073–H	Reinhold Steinbeck		
		073–BG	Reinhold Steinbeck	084–H	Yvonne Martin Rygiert
		075–H	Maria Camacho	084–L	Yvonne Martin Rygiert
		075–BG	Reinhold Steinbeck	084–C	Yvonne Martin Rygiert
		076–H	Carlos Serrano	084–R	Yvonne Martin Rygiert
		076–B	Tamara Carleton	085	Anders Häggman
		077–H	LinkedIn.com Christophe Vetterli personal page		
067–M	"Modernizing the Paper Notebook for the Digital Age" report, 2012, ME310 digital collection, Stanford Libraries, http://purl.stanford.edu/wd685zw8578			### 1960s	
		077–BG	University of St.Gallen MBA (@unisgmba), Instagram photo	088	James L. Adams Papers (SC0949), Department of Special Collections & University Archives, Stanford Libraries
		078–H	Falk Uebernickel	090–H	Gary Anderson
		078–BG	Goodpatch Europe (@goodpatcheurope), Instagram.com photo	090–BG	Warren Seering

1970s

092–H Warren Seering

092–BG Warren Seering
093* Warren Seering
 [enhanced using resources provided by www.veila.com]
094–H Tim Hight
094–B Tim Hight
095–H Stanford University School of Engineering faculty page
095–L* "Microfiche auto-indexer" report, 1976, Mechanical Engineering– 310 digital collection, Stanford Libraries, https://searchworks.stanford.edu/view/9527932 *[enhanced using resources provided by lstore.graphics]*
095–R* ibid.
096–L Tom Cooper
096–C LinkedIn.com Jeff Lotz personal page
096–R LinkedIn.com Laird Cagan personal page
097–L* "Portable telephone" report, 1980, Mechanical Engineering– 310 digital collection, Stanford Libraries, https://searchworks.stanford.edu/view/9527943 *[enhanced using resources provided by lstore.graphics]*
097–R* ibid.
098* "The para-bike" report, 1980, Mechanical Engineering-310 digital collection, Stanford Libraries, https://searchworks.stanford.edu/view/9527945 *[enhanced using resources provided by lstore.graphics]*

1980s

100–H https://edu.qq.com/a/20180104/010537.htm
100–BG "Robot fixture for precise drilling" report, 1984, Mechanical Engineering– 310 digital collection, Stanford Libraries, https://searchworks.stanford.edu/view/9527981
101 Eric Byler
102–H LinkedIn.com David Cannon personal page
102–BG Stanford Center for Professional Development, "ME210: An Experience in Product-Based Learning" video still, 1997
104–H LinkedIn.com Ade Mabogunje personal page
104–BG Larry Leifer
106 Tyler Bushnell
107–H Vinod Baya
107–BG Vinod Baya
108 Vinod Baya

1990s

110–H LinkedIn.com Darren Bonnstetter personal page
110–BG "Support system for walking rehabilitation patients" report, 1991, Mechanical Engineering-310 digital collection, Stanford Libraries, https://searchworks.stanford.edu/view/9528062
111–L* "Support system for walking rehabilitation patients" report, 1991, Mechanical Engineering-310 digital collection, Stanford Libraries, https://searchworks.stanford.edu/view/9528062 *[enhanced using resources provided by Antoniu at fuzzimo.com]*
111–R* ibid.
112–H Rafay Khan
112–BG "Apple cooling" report, 1990, Mechanical Engineering-310 digital collection, Stanford Libraries, https://searchworks.stanford.edu/view/9528043

113*   Stanford Daily, volume 200, issue 62, 22 January 1992 [enhanced using resources provided by graphicsfuel.com]
114–H   LinkedIn.com Kreig Ecklund personal page
114–BG   "Thermosiphon assembly for high-powered microprocessors" report, 1993, Mechanical Engineering-310 digital collection, Stanford Libraries, https://searchworks.stanford.edu/view/9528077
115–H   LinkedIn.com Sami Bitar personal page
115–BG   "Double-ended pressure regulator" report, 1995, Mechanical Engineering-310 digital collection, Stanford Libraries, https://searchworks.stanford.edu/view/9528110
116–H   LinkedIn.com Maria Yang personal page
116–B*   Stanford Center for Professional Development, "ME210: An Experience in Product-Based Learning" video still, 1997 [enhanced using resources provided by Victor A at be.net/lovecoffeemusic]
117–T   LinkedIn.com Sam Yen personal page
117–B   LinkedIn.com Jesse Adams personal page
118–HL   LinkedIn.com Gabriel Aldaz personal page
118–HR   LinkedIn.com Alex Asseily personal page
118–BG   Gabriel Aldaz
119–T   Gabriel Aldaz
119–H   LinkedIn.com Craig Litherland personal page
120–H   www.owsleybrownpresents.com/team
120–B*   Stanford Center for Professional Development, "ME210: An Experience in Product-Based Learning" video, 1997 [enhanced using resources provided by mrmockup.com]
121–H   LinkedIn.com Lawrence Neeley personal page
121–B*   Stanford Center for Professional Development, "ME210: An Experience in Product-Based Learning" video still, 1997 [enhanced using resources provided by Daniel Gomes de Souza at behance.net]

2000s

122   Anders Häggman
124*   Mark Cutkosky, "Developments in (global) project-based design education" presentation slides, 2000 [enhanced using resources provided by Marcin Wichary at guidebookgallery.org]
125–H   Becky Currano
125–BG   Stanford Center for Design Research web archives
126–H   LinkedIn.com Philipp Skogstad personal page
126–BG   "Optimum human machine interface for the IT generation" report, 2004, Mechanical Engineering-310 digital collection, Stanford Libraries, https://searchworks.stanford.edu/view/9528176
127–H   LinkedIn.com Neeraj Sonalkar personal page
127–BG   Neeraj Sonalkar
128–H   Sushi Suzuki
128–BG   "Improving the open air experience" report, 2005, Mechanical Engineering-310 digital collection, Stanford Libraries, https://searchworks.stanford.edu/view/9528182

129–L	"Improving the open air experience" report, 2005, Mechanical Engineering-310 digital collection, Stanford Libraries, https://searchworks.stanford.edu/view/9528182		139–BG	"TESIS" report, 2010, Universidad Nacional Autónoma De México		

129–L "Improving the open air experience" report, 2005, Mechanical Engineering-310 digital collection, Stanford Libraries, https://searchworks.stanford.edu/view/9528182
129–C ibid.
129–R ibid.
130–T LinkedIn.com Mark Bianco personal page
130–B LinkedIn.com Micah Lande personal page
131–T LinkedIn.com Dan Manian personal page
131–B Santhi Analytis
132–H LinkedIn.com Jackie Bernhelm personal page
132–B Yanran Lu
133–H LinkedIn.com Lindsey Sunden personal page
133–B Lindsey Sunden
134–H LinkedIn.com Miika Heikkinen personal page
134–BG Miika Heikkinen
134–B Miika Heikkinen
135–ALL Miika Heikkinen
136–H Anders Häggman
136–BG Anders Häggman
136–B Anders Häggman
137 Anders Häggman
138–T LinkedIn.com Josh Carter personal page
138–B LinkedIn.com Brandon Richardson personal page
139–H LinkedIn.com Bryan Duggan personal page

139–BG "TESIS" report, 2010, Universidad Nacional Autónoma De México
140–H LinkedIn.com Chris Pell personal page
140–BG "Audi Interact" report, 2010, ME310 project archives, Stanford University
141–H LinkedIn.com Mark Schar personal page
141–BG Mark Schar
142–H LinkedIn.com Tim Wong personal page
142–BG Mark Schar

2010s

144–T Tyler Bushnell
144–B LinkedIn.com Alexandre Jais personal page
145–H LinkedIn.com Tatiana Salazar personal page
145–BG Tatiana Salazar Londoño
146 Tatiana Salazar Londoño
147–H Yong Lin
147–B* "Team El Pais Final Project Report", 2012, Mechanical Engineering-310 digital collection, Stanford Libraries, https://searchworks.stanford.edu/view/kz399yh9465 *[enhanced using resources provided by lstore.graphics]*
148–H LinkedIn.com Teresa Tombelli personal page
148–BG Teresa Tombelli
149 Anders Häggman

Course Listings

152 Tamara Carleton
154 Stanford University Registrar
155–T ibid.
155–B ibid.
156–T ibid.
156–B ibid.
157 ibid.
158 ibid.
159 ibid.
160 ibid.
161 ibid.

Lexicon

162 Anders Häggman
165 Center for Design Research archives, Stanford University

Publications

166 Anders Häggman

Network Maps

174 Anders Häggman
176 Sushi Suzuki
177 Sushi Suzuki
178 Sushi Suzuki
179 Sushi Suzuki
180 ME310 course archives, Stanford University
181-187 ibid.

Image Sources

194 Anders Häggman

Thank You

A big thank you goes to all the Stanford ME310 alumni and other contributors who generously shared their stories for this book.

I am also grateful for the support and notes from several Stanford University faculty involved with the class over the years — notably Jim Adams, Larry Leifer, Mark Cutkosky, and George Toye.

I also owe special thanks to the lovely graphic design efforts of Brent Campbell for the template and to the tireless efforts of ME310 alum Anders Häggman for the book's final layout and polish.

Also thanks to Andrew Goddard, Zac Farrow, and Bill Cockayne for the extra data support and fact checking.

Hopefully, any errors are few, and the stories of ME310 live on. — *Editor*

www.ingramcontent.com/pod-product-compliance
Lightning Source LLC
Chambersburg PA
CBHW051351070526
44584CB00025B/3719